The Insanity Of Humanity

DAVID COLES

Copyright © David Coles 2014

The right of David Coles to be identified as the author of this work has been asserted in accordance with the Copyright, Designs and Patents Act of 1988.

All rights reserved.

Owing to the delicate nature of the information I share, I would prefer that no part of this book is reproduced or transmitted in any form or by any means, electronic or mechanical, including photocopying, recording or by any information storage and retrieval system, without prior permission in writing from the publisher. However, in a world of advanced technology and information sharing, this is obviously expensive and time consuming to enforce, so my request is out of respect for my life's journey and for your own integrity.

First published in 2014

David Coles is a human behaviour expert and creator of Life Expansion Technique - a highly advanced system of life guidance.

Please visit David's website at:

thevegancounsellor.com

ISBN 978-0-9942182-0-9

Forward

My sister passed away in October 2009. She faced the most painful, perceptually challenging and soul-destroying reality that I have ever personally seen another human being endure. In the last year of her life the disabling effects of her cancer left her physically immobilised and emotionally depleted. She used to say to me that she felt completely useless because she could no longer care for her young children or husband anymore. I told her that she was far from useless, in fact I told her something very different. I shared with her that she, more than anyone I had ever known, inspired me to be bigger than anything life throws at me ... to never accept any drama in this world and face it all as honestly and bravely as I can. She encouraged me, even in her darkest moments, to continue the journey that I had been on since a child - to unravel the challenges of existence that lay in front of us all, to step out of any restrictive learning that my mind had absorbed, and take on life's information without ever looking backwards; which required me to be in a place of no editing, staying completely harmonious with all I experienced. In doing this a massive realisation opened up for me; the idea of living in a permanently expansive state, so you are always bigger and more powerful than anything you encounter. I found the key to accomplish such a thing was to unleash my compassion completely beyond anything pertaining to my personal life. And that I did! In doing so I freed up my intelligence, creativity and my ability to feel life.

I became bigger than my life story.

This book is dedicated to her life and all living creatures that have suffered as a consequence of blind human indulgence. I now realise it is possible for life to be expressed and created without the pain that pervades the human mind, and all the cruelty that this allows.

I write with love in my heart for all living beings, but I will never accept that the destruction of one life to maintain another is a necessary component of human existence. So you may find my work confronting at times, as this is necessary if you are to look at what we all avoid in the journey of our species. If the collective human consciousness were not in a state of denial, then there would be no need for this book.

Please enjoy the ideas created from this phase of my life and look at it as a launching pad to expand your awareness. Expanding your reality is the key for an individual to grow beyond the disabling effects of anxiety and depression, and it is the key for the survival of our species if we are to unite once and for all.

Contents

INTRODUCTION	1

PHASE ONE

LIFE OR SOMETHING LIKE IT!	13
So . . . where are we?	18
Insane or not insane, that is the question!	26
Background intelligence	28
The cure is?	29

PHASE TWO

PAIN'S DOMAIN	33
The ~~twilight~~ pain zone	35
The evolution of Pain's Domain	37
The Pain - Human Combo Deal	38
The entry point of Conscious Energy	40
Driving school	44
Skipping classes	45
Blind in the midst of our own intelligence	46

PHASE THREE

IS PAIN THE KEY TO OUR FREEDOM?	51
The mechanisms of pain	52

Is it all just a dream?	53
The potential purpose of pain	54
A merger of intellectual systems	55
A mergence of darkness and light	56
Mercy please!	56
Pain is like a virus	57
Detoxifying your mind	58
The reservoir of pain	59
The beast!	61
Sharing the rage behind our beliefs	64
Call 911 we have an emergency!	64
To summarise...	65

PHASE FOUR

THE PROBLEM-SOLVING MIND	**67**
What is the Problem-Solving Mind?	69
A glitch in the system	72
It's not a problem	75
Really, it's not a problem!	77
Life misreading life	78
Untapped creative cyber genius	80
Isn't my perception my truth?	82
My problems are real!	86
Surely we are improving	92

PHASE FIVE

IN THE MIND OF A BABY	93
From the beginning	95
Bring it on!	100
Blinded by fear	102

PHASE SIX

THE CONSTRUCT	105
Welcome to the Construct . . .	107
Pinhole Theory	113
The Game	116
Emotions and the subconscious world	120

PHASE SEVEN

BEHIND CYBER WORLD	123
Pulling the mask off to expose The Ego	124
Cyber Selves	128
It can be seen	130
Putting the pieces together	134

PHASE EIGHT

THE NEED TO BELIEVE	137
I believe!	138
What is a belief?	139

Beliefs dissolve the truth	143
Are you talking to me!	144
The appearance of selfishness	145
A chink in the armour	146

PHASE NINE

A GLOBAL STATE OF INSANITY	151
Is humanity being sacrificed?	153
Corruption	160
She is a witch!	161
Trading integrity for control	165

PHASE TEN

PAIN COLLECTION MACHINES	169
Global amassing of pain	170
She screamed for help but nobody responded	170
Good versus evil	180

PHASE ELEVEN

THE INFORMATION SUPER-HIGHWAY	185
Is information power?	186
Waiting at the GoBus stop	190

PHASE TWELVE

WHAT'S IN IT FOR ME?	195
Wanting as a survival pathway	197
Walking a tight rope	200
Like pieces of the puzzle	201
Wanting is dangerous	202
Playing it safe	204
The law of diminishing returns	204

PHASE THIRTEEN

I NEED TO BE MORE!	207
Wanting to be something	208
To be or not to be - is not a fictional question!	209
Time is an illusion	211
When wanting becomes obsessive	215
Dream chasers	216
The mother-ship of anxiety	217
To surmise	218

PHASE FOURTEEN

NATURE'S INTENTION	221
So what was nature's intention?	223
Nature's weapon	226
Imagine a wolf cub	227

The dart theory	229
Life in a room	231
The loop of unsolvable disturbance	233
Prince or pauper?	235
Thoughts, emotions and survival	236
Collateral damage and the Pinhole Theory reviewed.	237
Fear is the guide	237

PHASE FIFTEEN

COLD CASE FILES	**239**
Opening the files	241
Living in the 'now'	241
'Now' versus 'What If'	246
Living in Isness	247
Emotions	249
Imagine if . . .	252
Opening up our sixth sense	253
Unified self	255
Life Speed Synchronisation	255

PHASE SIXTEEN

AWARENESS - SCIENCE OR MAGIC?	**257**
Awareness is freedom	259
Awareness creates	259
The science of awareness is magic!	260

My journey of awareness	261
Where have all of the wise elders gone?	263
Respect for all life	264
Caged in a world of control and pain	266
Can awareness be lonely?	267
Enter the Problem-Solving Mind	268
Let the adventure begin	269
Obstacle to awareness	270
Mourning the loss of beliefs	271
Is letting go cold and heartless?	274
Knowledge versus knowing	275

CONCLUSION

UTOPIA	281

Introduction

The Insanity of Humanity is the beginning of my personal investigation into the current status of human behaviour. This book was my first attempt to describe in writing what I was witnessing within my own existence and within those around me. Many years later, all I discovered still holds true for me, hence I decided to publish this book and make it available for others to share. Although my ability to express what I see has advanced dramatically, as has my ability to explore beyond what restricts my existence, I strongly suggest that this book offers an essential foundation of learning for anyone interested in finding peace in their world and the world we all share.

I am on an ongoing investigation to aid in the challenge of unravelling the mysterious experience we call life and to inspire humanity to think beyond what we currently consider is real; for if we do not, our opportunity to evolve into advanced and compassionate beings will be gone forever.

Let me ask, when you began your search for a book, were you looking for answers to finding happiness, confidence and inner peace? The human race has been chasing such things for many thousands of years, so why haven't we found them by now?

My suggestion is that we stop looking for what we don't have and start focusing our attention on what we do have, including the emotions that we perceive to be unpleasant or undesirable. The crisis in consciousness that we are currently experiencing is the necessary ingredient for inspiring us to wake up in the midst of the pain that controls our lives. The journey into the evolution of consciousness is alive and available for all who are willing. This book, if read with patience, an open mind and reflection upon ourselves and the societies we live in, provides a launching pad to unleash our experience of life beyond the constraints of fear, into a world of possibilities.

Do we know why, despite many thousands of years of transference of wisdom from generation to generation, that overall, we seem no closer to knowing why we do what we do? In fact, behind our reinforced masks of happiness and success, it would appear that we are all more disturbed and confused than ever. In addition, this innate programmed confusion is affecting every decision we make and therefore everything we create, including the structures of the societies we live in.

Surely, this must breathe life into the following questions:

What is this experience we call life?

Why is it so hard to stay feeling good?

Why do we need laws and physical enforcement to control our behaviour?

Why is anxiety and depression becoming a growing phenomenon within our youth and adults alike?

To answer these questions and free up the possibility of expanding and redirecting our experience of life, we need to first understand the precise nature of what it is that has created this perceptual reality that we exist in. If we were supposed to be permanently feeling good then we already would be, and there would be no need for this book.

I don't know about you, but the status of human functioning and the societies we have created do not appeal to my sensibilities of integrity and human decency. I have devoted my life to unravelling the mystery of what it is that keeps us trapped in an eternal state of misunderstood insanity – a condition that disallows us from admitting the truth as to the nature of our own behaviour. Just to face the truth of this could embark anyone on a life changing experience.

So let's start by exploring some simple observations of human functioning:

How do you feel right now?

INTRODUCTION

Ten minutes ago?

Yesterday?

Have you noticed how difficult it is to stay in one emotion, one way of feeling about life? Yet it is through our emotions that we experience life. And therefore it is through our emotions that we create our notion of self and the world in which we exist. So given the ever changing emotions we experience, it is obviously quite a challenge to hold onto any clear sense of self and life.

Look at this notion of self we create as an ever-changing expression of our conceptual world, however evolved a stage it may be at. So it would be reasonable to propose, as things currently stand, that we *are* what we experience; not just the picture we create of ourselves in this world, but the whole thing.

I mean everything!

People often limit their experience of life by seeing themselves as separate from life, as a human body looking out at the world. However, our brain is creating the complete realm of what we see – we are effectively looking at the inside of our mind. This realm develops meaning through a process of cleverly crafted thoughts and visual images, and these thoughts create various emotions.

And without the emotional component the experience would be . . . well, it would not be an experience.

Not yet anyway!

And without awareness, emotions control our ability to explore and experience beyond what we think life is. A notion that is currently quite limited to the parameters of survival. How we express our emotions heavily influences everything we live for, search for, question, problem-solve, chase and even become addicted to. Our emotional realm represents the outcome of our experiences, which is the outcome of us. So to 'work out' who you are in this realm is very confusing as it is forever changing.

Think about the societies we live in.

On this planet, we have created systems of functioning that tell us what we should feel, how we should express our feelings, when we should express them and what levels of expression are appropriate depending on the circumstances. So we have created a system that confines our emotional realm, which therefore restricts our experience of life, our intelligence and our creativity.

So how do you live your life? Do you freely express your feelings with confidence and clarity?

Given the current status of human functioning - probably not!

If that is the case you will never feel whole, you will never understand what life is and what you are within it. How could you when you are only feeling a small portion of it? You will die lost in a world of confused, distorted and constrained thoughts and corresponding feelings.

To understand life is to learn how to freely express emotions from a place of awareness and integrity, not fear! This can only happen once you understand your mind, the energy that guides it and what *you are* inside this experience. And to understand that energy will release you from the cage of thought that is currently restricting your existence.

Now, here is where things get a little tricky. The energy that guides us is the reason why finding ongoing happiness is almost impossible. But the good news is - its existence is not some big hidden secret. It is there for any of us to observe should we take the time to do so.

This energy is what we currently define as pain - the creator of our fears. We have been so programmed to react to pain that we've never devoted enough energy into understanding it. Understanding pain is essential in the exploration of the human mind, the physical realm, scientific research, psychology,

INTRODUCTION

spirituality and all that we experience. We see pain as something that we feel, rather than something that is guiding, via our minds, the creation of a world that resembles the essence of what it is. And it creates, also within our minds, masterful illusions to lure us into believing that our lives are more restricted than they really are. Pain restricts our emotions and guides them down a predictable, focused and narrow pathway that holds these illusions together. And whilst on this narrow path we cannot see the entirety of life, just portions of it - at least in terms of how we can feel it.

We are in a permanent state of conflict with something, each other, and within ourselves; hence we remain in a reactive place rather than an empowered one. So our current experience of life is an expression of whatever pain is. And if pain is the energy influencing the creation of the world we are experiencing, then I would suggest that we start getting to know it better.

But how do we get to know pain, particularly when we are supposedly programmed to avoid it at all cost? In simple terms, we do it by exploring and expanding our thoughts and feelings without limiting them to the story of humanity, to the story of us!

And how do we do that? By first waking up and embarking on a journey of awareness to expand our perception of what is. By expanding our thoughts we expand the experiential universe that we live in, and hence we feel more. When we feel more we inject more integrity into our lives. Then with appropriate guidance we know more. And in knowing more we open ourselves to the infinite possibilities of our existence. We then become the essence of what possibility represents - a new language of life that will progressively open our thoughts and emotions, unleashing our intelligence, creativity and compassion.

However, as things stand, every emotion is in fact an expression of pain, an expression of the dimension within which we exist. We are continuing to create a repressed version of life; hence we have a repressed experience of life. We therefore live in a repressed emotional state, which creates a repressed understanding of our existence. This repression creates intense pain. And the more intense the pain gets the more we will trade our integrity to gain control. It is through these distorted emotions that we are guiding the journey of the human species. We are creating a world that is going to become a living hell, yet technology, advertising campaigns, the laws we create, government controls, and the manipulation of information via various types of media, would lure us into believing that we are actually progressing in a healthy direction.

I will present to you something very different.

I have discovered that we are trapped and lost in The Insanity of Humanity; a dimension where consciousness is expressed through misunderstood pain. The feeling we know as fear, creates outcomes that we neither truly understand nor know how to respond to. The Insanity of Humanity, once fully understood, actually represents a window, a portal to another realm of existence. So pain, albeit unpleasant, is drawing our attention to look at life. Once you are looking, pain is no longer necessary and this is your moment to expand beyond it.

Try not to spend any time defending what is; the key to this portal is hidden in facing aspects of our existence that we seem to conveniently ignore or defend the most. These aspects are the less desirable characteristics of human behaviour; the ones we have decided are qualities of a poorly behaved minority. However, I am proposing that these qualities are within all of us, whether they are exposed or not, and it is time to truly look at human behaviour as it will guide us to something much greater.

Life is a challenge but far from a futile one. It is designed to ensure that only complete and expansive awareness, imbued with compassion, can ever find its way through this cleverly crafted maze of information.

Expanding the scene...

INTRODUCTION

If we keep repressing our feelings within the increasing controls and constraints that are being created by society, we will eventually have a very limited range of emotional expression and all the beauty of humanity will die. Why? Because beautiful emotions of genuine love and compassion are expansive feelings that embrace all that is. However, when trapped in a world of pain they will only be felt and shared in a distorted and manipulative sense. The further we continue to repress our ability to share our feelings in an honest manner, the more likely it is that the beauty that lies within us all will not be accessible to anyone.

So let's further understand how this happened and what we can do to change it.

It has been a long and arduous journey for the human species to reach the current phase of existence that we are experiencing today. We have certainly evolved in our ability to manipulate our environment, but it would appear that we are still confused as to how our minds work and the true nature of what forces are guiding our existence.

Psychological disturbance is rising amongst all of us, as we seem to be steering life on planet Earth towards a world of illusionary control, while we are in fact spiralling out of control. And we are using our mastery of technology to keep us safe from our fears, which is inadvertently controlling our lives. As increasing controls are put in place to supposedly protect us, our personal experience of life is shrinking, hence increasing our pain and reducing our ability to grow wiser from it.

Individually and collectively, this process is convincing us that we should continue to run from our pain by chasing the false lure of happiness! Yet in reality, it is pain that is guiding us towards its destiny of control. There is no happiness at the end of this tunnel, only darkness - a world of alienation, where our chance to liberate our existence beyond the Insanity of Humanity will be gone forever. This chance however is still alive today, so let's not waste any more time!

This book is a wake up call for *humanity*.

And for any individual that has had enough of letting disabling pain consume their existence! Look at the term humanity, not as a description of what we are, but rather what we have the potential to become.

The Insanity of Humanity is reflected in our inability to effectively deal with the worldwide crises we are confronted with – whether that be Depression, Terrorism, Human and Animal Slavery or Global Warming; a state of affairs that we all created during the collective process of sharing our pain infused thoughts and emotions

It is time to face and understand the mechanisms of the human mind that has created everything that we are resisting and trying to change for our survival.

It is time to stop surviving, wake up and start living!

If you have a desire to understand how your mind works, and how it influences the shaping of your life and the world in which you exist, then you have entered a realm of learning that will potentially transform your entire experience of what life is.

I invite you to join me on a voyage of awareness towards understanding the world of illusion that we are all trapped in. This illusion creates a distorted, confusing and disturbing version of reality. We are enforcing this illusion onto all we encounter as if it is real, and our lack of awareness that this is happening is what creates The Insanity of Humanity.

Although I offer a practical pathway out of the insanity that is pervading our minds, it is essential for all of us to face the truth of our behaviour, and to stop painting a picture of humanity that is a glorious version of what it actually is. We are all constantly trading our integrity for the need to feel in control, to attain a

INTRODUCTION

notion of happiness and achievement. Yet, we still somehow expect that life should reward us, despite our lack of honesty.

Let's earn the right to be happy, to celebrate humanity and sit in a place of joyful bliss!

If you think what I say is negative and therefore do not like it, then you are lost in your life story and the story of humanity, and resisting what is! You are lost in a purpose-built mechanism that is guiding you towards a world of negativity, all in the disguise of positive thinking and integrity - a world I refer to as Pain's Domain. The positive thinking which we all chase is a false lure created by a cleverly crafted system of thoughts and emotions.

We are in a system that ensures the continuance of the pathways of pain.

Why?

Because pain created it.

There can be nothing else if we continue to defend and protect our distorted sense of self.

And what guides us to do this?

PAIN!

Pain is a system of communication. Think of it as the energy that guides the creation of all that we are and all that we experience. Although pain creates a predictable reality, it is not stagnant – it is constantly changing, hence we all need to be observing it and thinking one step ahead of it.

As a species, we have been attempting to liberate our existence from the pain that clouds our minds for a long time. In this process, we have somehow managed to alienate ourselves further from what it is we seek. It is certainly human nature to seek. Nevertheless, it would appear that this quality is not helping us to find genuine happiness. The key to our freedom seems to be well hidden from our view.

So what is seeking?

Effectively it is problem-solving. So we have problem-solved our way into our current situation and now we are trying to problem-solve our way out of it. What makes us think that the manner in which we have been functioning throughout the history of our existence, is suddenly going to turn around and start working for us? Firstly, we know no other way. Secondly, we are convinced that our salvation lies just beyond the next problem to solve.

Problem-solving is a mode of functioning that our minds have always been, and continue to operate in. In fact, our ability to solve problems is how we survived as a species.

So, if problem-solving got us this far, why can't we just keep doing what we have always done?

The answer is quite straightforward. There is one very interesting but largely overlooked glitch in this system - as a problem-solver you can never be satisfied, or you wouldn't bother to solve problems in the first place! And to top it all off, this mode of functioning was created by pain as a guide for decision-making.

So how can we find permanent happiness when we are using pain as our guide?

There is a simple answer to that too.

We can't!

Another unfortunate characteristic of the problem-solving mode is that pain gets transferred from one mind to another and from generation to generation. Hence, it keeps growing in intensity within our minds both individually and collectively over time.

INTRODUCTION

This escalating pain leads us to dig deeper into our problem-solving pathways.

Why?

Because the more pain we feel, the more life feels like a problem. Of course this just leads to more pain and then more problem-solving and so on it goes - and we wonder why we feel so stressed, perplexed and insecure most of the time.

So here we all are. Sitting together on planet Earth, all feeling psychologically disabled, yet forever living for our dreams that are lost in a world of confusion. This leaves us looking out into the unknown with nothing but our pain and the fear that this creates. We are waiting for something that does not exist; not knowing how to embrace the truth that our salvation exists not in front of us, but within us.

> **Our compassion will be our saviour.**

So if liberation from your pain is your desire, then I must tell you all I have to offer is the truth!

> **Be mindful that the truth can't hurt you, only your resistance to it.**

We are lost and effectively asleep in a dimension that is governed by rules and regulations, whether they are those imposed by nature or by ourselves – which is in fact one and the same thing. We have become so heavily reliant upon the very systems that imprison us that we reluctantly open our minds to explore beyond this. This denial allows for all of the convenient justifications of our behaviour that we use to disguise our lack of integrity.

Our challenge is to move beyond these restrictive parameters that incarcerate our existence, and take the human spirit into a realm we have never travelled. It is time for all of us to unite as pioneers and head fearlessly into a new world of existence - a world that can only be seen if we look beyond the superficial layers of our falsely identified place of security.

This notion of security is housed within our beliefs. We attempt to find freedom within this structure without recognising that the need for security displaces the possibility of feeling free. When we are chasing freedom, we are simply chasing the idea of bringing tangible meaning into our lives. However, in our search for meaning we get stuck in the sensation that life is a problem that needs solving. As long as we see anything as a problem, our lives will never feel secure or make sense

Life can never be solved as such, because as soon as we know something, effectively we know nothing.

Why?

Because life is always new and forever changing. It can't be held to definable boundaries. We can learn to flow with this reality only when we function beyond the confines of the world that pain creates in our minds.

I welcome you to come with me on a journey into The Insanity of Humanity.

To liberate the human mind beyond our insatiable fear-driven need for happiness and security!

PHASE ONE

Life or something like it!

I live to feel, to experience more, yet it is my feelings that I disguise in a riddle, a lie that I cannot understand, even though I created it.

Well at least I think I did. So no matter what I do, I end up feeling less, which always leaves me lost in one feeling - confusion!

So, what is going on in this world of ours?

PHASE ONE

I feel lonely.

I feel scared.

I feel disillusioned.

I feel absolutely miserable!

But it is not a problem.

How could it not be a problem to feel this way?

Because it is normal to be unhappy!

So, don't feel odd or different. We are all experiencing various levels of psychological pain, confusion, disturbance, insecurity and anxiety, whether we admit it or not! And those who claim not to be feeling such things are probably those who are maintaining a false sense of power by controlling other living beings and by not facing the cruelty inflicted as a consequence of their behaviour.

There is no such thing as a permanent state of positive thinking, happiness or enlightenment in our current mode of existence.

Why?

Because it is human nature to solve problems.

In fact, it was the key to our survival. Problem-solving creates a very narrow and focussed mode of existence whilst projecting desires into the future. And we exist within that mode, hence never experiencing anything other than a small and distorted aspect of life. What does this mean? Are we destined to never feel good? Or is it possible that we could all live another way?

Yes it is possible!

But we will be living, functioning and experiencing life in a way that is totally different from what we have become addicted to and reliant upon.

Our priority is to first understand the true nature of our existence and what lies behind the surprising and sometimes confusing consequences of being highly advanced problem-solvers.

So . . . where are we?

We are effectively all living in a box!

We are living in a box with walls that are made of intertwined fear based thoughts that represent our entire existence.

These thoughts develop and maintain our belief structure. Moreover, this belief structure represents the walls of the box.

Within these walls is our life story - one narrow, finite and minute pathway of experiences from which we create our notion of self; a notion that we spend our life running from, yet desperately protecting at the same time.

So each belief represents one bar in the prison of our minds!

Life or something like it!

Look through the following list of words:

Honesty
Tranquillity
Acceptance

Trust
Loyalty
Happiness

Courtesy
Kindness
Contentment

Wisdom
Balance
Enlightenment

Joy
Hope
Excitement

Strength
Forthrightness
Confidence

Truth
Integrity
Love

Respect
Compassion
World Peace

PHASE ONE

Now look through this list of words:

Fear
Corruption
Racism

Contempt
Infidelity
Divorce

Stress
Road rage
Cruelty

Drugs
Addictions
Eating disorders

Sadness
Hopelessness
Depression

Pain
Insecurity
Suicide

Anxiety
Panic attacks
Psychological disorders

Terrorism
Global Warming
Mass hysteria

Do any of these conditions / emotions / issues sound familiar?

Which list contains words that embody the greater part of our existence and the world in which we live?

In the second list is there one, several, or enough to make you feel insane?

Why have the words from the second list come to describe realities consistently present in the lives of so many people? Even more importantly, why do the words in the first list so rarely apply to our lives, other than in our dreams?

Take a moment to pause and reflect.

Our problem-solving minds focus our attention on the second list as we see them as obstacles preventing us from attaining the qualities embodied in the first list. We do this without realising that this approach is what is creating the scenario that we are trying to change. So the life force behind the words in the second list is growing in size and intensity over time, and the energy in the words from the first is becoming further removed from our grasp.

In addition, did you notice whether you felt a greater emotional response while reading the second list?

If so, this is quite normal, given that our minds are always on the lookout for any threats to our well-being. As much as we want our lives to embody the words from the first list, they are not as necessary for our survival. We see it this way because we are stuck in a problem-solving mode that ultimately has the objective of prolonging our individual lives. In this process of trying to avoid death, we stay motivated by chasing happiness.

But it was never about being happy – just surviving!

Emotions attached to anything in the first list are like a mystical lure created by pain to keep the process of evolution alive, which keeps us alive, which increases the likelihood of the survival of our species. But it also allows for enormous amounts of corruption in human behaviour; it leaves us constantly dwelling on our own pain and hence avoiding the pain of what we see around us. And this leads to all the cruelty that we partake in but seem incapable of seeing as something we are doing – even whilst doing it. Like, for example, the abuse of poor innocent animals that we breed and kill in the millions every single day. Even putting their dead body parts in our mouths does not give a clue that something is not right - very strange hey?

We are in a survival mode that keeps the brain prioritising where its attention should be focussed based on its construct of learning. For example, although it is seen as a problem not to be happy, it is seen as a greater problem to not be depressed. Hence, we are building a world that resembles where our predominant focus of thought lies. Although we do not want to be depressed, it is our fear of depression that creates the corruption in our minds that ensures the inevitability of it occurring. So it won't be long before depression will be an epidemic in our societies. Then we will see it as an even bigger problem!

Problem-solving as a pathway for dealing with life actually creates more problems than we started with.

And not just more problems, but bigger and more elaborate ones - keeping the illusion alive that life itself is a problem.

The truth we can learn is that depression, or any other of the words from the second list, are not the issues to be observing. They are just outcomes, by-products of functioning from within our Construct of learning– the psychological box that creates our life story.

This is all part of how learning works – it creates a brilliant illusion that stops us from seeing the truth as to what is controlling our existence. This illusion keeps us chasing happiness by problem-solving what lies between our desperately desired emotional state and us. So although it feels like we are focussed on the 'positive', subconsciously we are always focussed on the 'negative' – the issues that we define as obstacles to getting to our chosen destination. Not surprising really, particularly when you consider that pain is our guide!

It is quite intriguing to observe how this pathway of thinking has developed the world that we are now living in. Global warming for example, did not just come out of nowhere; it is a physical manifestation of human behaviour when functioning as we currently do.

It seems insane doesn't it?

The less we want depression, terrorism or global warming, the more we will fear them. And the more we fear them the more likely it is that these or similar conditions will occur. This is because we put so much fear-imbued focus and attention on it. This theoretical observation applies to our whole existence and thus it applies to all of the issues that I have mentioned - including the first list. For example, the more we want happiness the more we fear not finding it, and therefore our focus is once again stuck in a problem-solving mode which negates happiness. This process is happening whether we are aware of it or not – defying the most persistent attempts to think positively.

It is essential that we understand the mechanisms of the mind leading us to function in such a manner. Otherwise, in the process of deciding that our topical issues of woe or desire are the key problems to solve, we will inadvertently ensure that we won't solve them.

Problem-solving appears to work because we have survived as a species to this point, but it is becoming glaringly obvious that we need to find another way to explore our existence – that is, beyond our obsessive and blinkered need to stay alive.

So why can't we just see this and stop it?

Because whilst functioning in a problem-solving mode we use pain and fear as a guide and fear distorts our ability to accurately see life – it narrows our vision of thought. To understand what it is that I am proposing requires open and lateral vision. Otherwise, our destiny is becoming very easy to predict – and it won't be pretty!

So our ability to read life accurately will continue to diminish as our determination to gain control of our lives rises.

Hence driving us closer and closer towards a psychological black hole within our minds.

Stop and think about these things: War, terrorism, famine, and environmental disaster. Based on what we witness in today's world and our inability individually or collectively to effectively do anything about them, it seems insane for us to continue in our current patterns of behaviour. It is important to be reminded that it was our current mode of thinking that created all this supposed chaos.

Maybe the people that we have labelled as insane are in fact closer to a place of sanity than we could have ever imagined! They are the ones who have stopped utilising and contributing to the very systems of functioning that are destroying us all.

However, before we diagnose our entire species as insane, let's try to get a little closer to the truth as to what is actually occurring.

Every word in the second list is an outcome of something. It was inevitable that these outcomes would occur; hence, they were unavoidable and therefore not wrong in the very nature of their existence. However, they will continue to occur with ever-increasing magnitudes of intensity if we don't teach ourselves how to understand and accept that they are simply a consequence of a certain mode of thinking. This mode of thinking denies the qualities in the first list from ever being a substantial part of the reality of our existence.

The creation of all the previously mentioned unwanted issues can be traced back through the logical pathways of the human mind, to expose that they were all fashioned from the same source.

All of the mayhem that we inflict upon this world and upon ourselves is being caused by a mechanism that is very predictable in the nature of its existence. Owing to this integral characteristic, this same mechanism has the potential to be transformed to such a degree, that not one single word on the second list would ever present itself to the human species as a problem ever again. They would only serve as reminders of past human functioning, so we would know where in the mind to never allow our thoughts to travel again.

Currently people are desperately scrambling to try to separate, categorise and control all of the undesirable realities of today's world, failing to recognize that they are all connected to the same thing. With this attitude, it doesn't matter what we do or how we go about it, as all solutions will be futile. The corrupt pathways of the mind that created the problems in the first place, will simply search out and find another avenue to express the pain and fear that is consuming all of humanity.

Whether you are an animal activist, an environmentalist, or a person trying to cope with anxiety and depression, ultimately your journey will unfortunately be one full of frustration and disappointment – at least until we, as a species, understand the mechanisms of functioning that are driving our thinking.

For example, if we curb our current processes of behaviour that are leading to the destruction of our environment, the fear that we share in order to develop the appropriate strategy to deal with this situation, will increase the power that pain has over our lives.

It is essential that we stop panicking about our current status and realise that until we remove ourselves from our world of distorted pain and fear, we are inadvertently feeding the very thing that is destroying us.

Insane or not insane, that is the question!

The Insanity of Humanity . . . for me this is a simple yet powerful combination of words. The thoughts provoked by these words give me much cause to pause and reflect on the reality of my existence and its influence on all things that cross my path.

I ask myself: Am I sane? Do I differ from the rest of humanity? Am I a better person? Is my way of thinking the superior way of thinking, or am I just caught up in the Insanity of Humanity like everybody else? Is it acceptable for me to enforce my way through life and accept the suffering that is created in the process of satisfying my need to feel good and survive?

Where do I draw the line? At what point has my behaviour gone too far and at too great a cost?

Has sacrifice in fact become an acceptable condition in the journey of the human species? Is it possible that a state of insanity is a prerequisite to our survival?

Perhaps it is *insanity* that has led us to the position of power and domination that we humans have over this planet.

The Insanity of Humanity in essence is our denial of our current modes of behaviour and the effects that they create. It is represented by our need to be seen in a light of purity while conveniently justifying our cruelty - as if this somehow negates the painful effects this will create within our minds.

We are therefore enforcing a distorted version onto life that creates undesirable outcomes, and then we try to solve these problems as if it wasn't us that created them in the first place.

In addition, here is the irony of it all; our blind obsession for survival could potentially be the catalyst for our inevitable demise - unless we discover a new way to exist.

A crucial starting point for humanity is to accept that we can't rely on the part of the brain that has created the very problems for which we seek answers to.

That would be as ludicrous as asking your enemy where they would suggest you could find a safe place to sleep tonight.

But that is exactly what we are doing.

Using pain as our guide, we have problem-solved our way into this mess and now we are trying to problem-solve our way out of it. And that I propose is insane!

The human species has throughout recorded history been caught in a world of drama and power struggles. Every era has had its 'problems' that are considered important or life threatening, requiring intense focus and attention. Humans created most of these problems in the first place, via the problem-solving pathways of their minds. Then in the process of finding solutions via the same pathways of thinking, new problems emerged. The issues we are facing today are no different, irrespective of what shape or form they appear – they have all evolved from this process of thinking.

Even if we successfully change business functioning to reduce greenhouse gases or even if we capture every known terrorist, it won't ensure our ongoing survival, it won't make us happy, it won't stop depression, it won't change the fact that we will create new problems to channel our fears into, and most importantly, it wont change the nature of the human brain.

If you want to a have a chat with a terrorist to understand what they are doing and thinking, then have a chat with your own mind; as it is terrorising your existence, holding you captive and using your integrity in exchange for power and control. This is leaving you lost in a world of pain, whilst you terrorise other living beings. Think about that. For example I know there are lots of people that would condone America's attempt to destroy anyone associated to terrorism. The justification is that they say they are getting the evil people in the world. But the supposed terrorists don't think they're evil, they think the Americans are; and the majority of people on both sides of this ugly coin want justice and security whilst quite happily accepting that animals are abused for their pleasure. So who is worse? It is all madness!

Can you see what I am saying?

If our planet and all of the animals on it could speak, they would certainly label us all as terrorists, as we are all enforcing our behaviour on this world while conveniently disguising our actions in denial and blame.

It's pain that drives our behaviour and misunderstood pain creates fear. It is a well-known statement that we create what we fear.

Think of what we currently fear as a species and then you can predict the future! Given that pain and fear drive us to solve problems, it is probably a good idea to stop seeing life as a problem to solve. Sounds simple enough - and it is and it will be, once we understand what drives our minds to think the way we currently do.

Background intelligence

Human thought is currently derived from an aspect of the brain, which I will be referring to as the Problem-Solving Mind.

Based on the previous list of undesirable outcomes, it may appear that we have grown increasingly ignorant and blind on our journey through life.

However, don't be fooled by the masterful mechanism that is controlling us.

The Problem-Solving Mind is an absolute genius and it is the creator and architect of our entire experience - it has created a parallel version of life that is so sophisticated that we erroneously believe it is real. In fact, it would appear that this aspect of the brain, which so profoundly guides and affects us, cannot and will not allow us to be free: not even in the face of the individual and planetary chaos that we witness daily in our lives. It even allows for good, loving and caring people to continue eating animals even though they know that suffering and cruelty is attached to their actions. That in itself is enough evidence we can use to inspire further investigation as to what the Problem-Solving Mind's objectives are!

The reason its so hard for me to be able to encourage people that they should give up their problem-solving pathways is because they think they are the Problem-Solving Mind – and this is all part of the illusion. There is an 'us' beyond all this that can fully embrace living without needing to see any aspects of life as a problem. Nevertheless, if you want to fight to defend problem-solving, go ahead, as I have heard numerous arguments and justifications as to why we must do so. That is all fine, but I hope you can handle the world that this is creating.

A world where inevitably there won't be any problems because we won't exist!

The cure is?

As a cure to our presently destructive modes of thinking, it would be very tempting to banish all of the selfish, cruel, controlling, dominating and blaming people from our world to another planet. However this technique would, if we were being honest, leave planet Earth inhabited by very few people, if any!

What if we had a choice to do otherwise?

An alternative would be to wake up to the reality that we are all contributing to this personal and global pathway of destruction. I suggest that together we all look beyond the superficial layers of our existence and explore deeper into the mechanisms of life. It can all be explained, it can all be understood, but to truly break free from what is keeping us trapped in the Insanity of Humanity, we must understand and sense what it is that is forcing us to hold on so desperately to our pain, our fear and our beliefs.

A new phase of human evolution is not a guarantee, just a possibility.

This possibility is given a higher probability of occurrence given the right guidance, awareness, expansion and integrity.

I have left much unexplained at this point. There is a lot to be un-learned and significantly more to be learned. I assure you that by the time you understand this book, the nature of your existence and all its influences will make a lot more sense. At the very least it will have embarked you on a journey to find out more - to see through the illusion.

For now, stop and consider: The term *humanity* is often used in connection with the concepts of kindness or compassion for others (including animals), and *insanity* is often used to reference a lack of reason or good sense, whereby people partake in extreme foolishness, or an act that demonstrates it.

Which of these two realms do you think we are closer to? Or have we always been insane and the consequences of this are simply something we can no longer avoid? If we are to look at insanity as a mode of thinking, feeling, surviving and experiencing life, then I would suggest that the answer is yes! Confronting but true, and together we can help each other get beyond the madness that pervades human thought.

Globally and individually we are all partaking in behaviour that demonstrates a lack of healthy reasoning, yet we continue to enforce our way despite the obvious evidence that is available for all to see; verification that we are trapped in a state of insanity.

To embrace what I present, so you can see whether it is embodied in truth or not, will require you to read and absorb this information without cross referencing it to any of your existing knowledge on life and human functioning; a necessary component of awareness if one is to find emotional freedom. Then once understood - compare away!

What is being proposed to you is not a condemnation of humanity, but rather the exposure of the possibility to expand into a place of existence where the term humanity will more aptly define what we are.

Sit back and take an honest look at the shared pathway that we have created together. The level of fear, control, destruction, cruelty, violence and psychological disturbance that we see on a mass level, is simply the accumulated end result of the interaction between all of our individual minds - an interaction of thought and emotions that allows pain to be the lifeblood of our existence.

Once we understand our minds and stop avoiding the truth of our behaviour, we will be well on our way to a realm of possibilities that I can only begin to imagine.

All I ask of you is that you read this book in its entirety before you jump to any conclusions. I am attempting to expose what has been brilliantly disguised throughout the history of human existence. Don't expect that this can be explained, understood or embraced easily. However, awareness of all I present is enough to begin the process of creating freedom from the psychological box in which we are all trapped.

It's time to stop and take a closer and more honest look inside all our minds.

PHASE TWO

Pain's Domain

PHASE TWO

Pain . . . I avoid it at all cost, yet I am curiously drawn to it to guide the journey of my life.

It is as if I am in some kind of trance from which I cannot wake.

The ~~twilight~~ pain zone

The journey of life on this planet from a human perspective sometimes feels like we are caught in the twilight zone - a sphere of experience that appears sinister or dangerous because of its uncertainty, unpredictability, or ambiguity.

If you really stop and think about it, being alive is a very strange experience. The evidence speaks strongly that we are going to die; yet we hold on so desperately to life without even really knowing what it is that we are holding on to. We don't even understand death or why we fear it so much. A lot of the time being 'awake' feels as disturbing as the nightmares we experience while asleep, let alone the fact that we don't really even know where we go when we are asleep.

It is quite normal to experience the sensation that something is not quite right. This feeling is embodied with a great deal of truth; however, we are unable to read behind this message because we focus on the sensation itself in a reactive manner. That is, we see this as a problem that needs solving and once again, we get lost in the limited story of our lives.

If we genuinely want to feel comfortable in the realm in which we exist, then it is important to create a greater understanding of what our journey is all about. Then we can start to understand how this interrelates with other aspects of life. To aid in this process I would suggest that we explore some of the key driving forces that are directing the behavioural characteristics of all living creatures, including us.

In this phase of the discussion the focus will be on one force in particular, one that has established a very solid position in the journey of life. If we want to truly understand what is going on in our minds, then come with me on a journey, not into what feels like the twilight zone, but into what it really is . . . the Pain Zone.

Pain has become one of the most powerful things influencing evolution, intelligence, awareness and consciousness. The incredible influencing power of pain is most readily witnessed when it is harnessed within the realms of sophisticated creations of life, such as human beings.

Whatever your background knowledge with regard to the topic of pain, I encourage you to put the majority of this learning to the side for now, and open your mind to seeing pain in a totally new light. Rather than just seeing pain as a sensation that you feel in response to an undesirable experience, try to see it as an energy that represents a mode of functioning that creates a certain style of survival for living creatures.

What I am exposing here, are the mechanisms behind the processes of pain rather than just focusing on the uncomfortable feeling of pain itself. In truly understanding these processes we can totally transform our existing concept of pain, the way that we currently experience it and consequently redirect our life out of the Insanity of Humanity.

Pain guides and influences the creation of everything we experience, thus if we understand pain we understand life (including where we are and what we have become). There is an intriguing message hidden deep within the realms of pain that can be decoded and understood, and to simply try and run away from it is certainly not the answer. Once decoded, it no longer becomes pain in the way we are currently experiencing it.

In general, when we feel great disturbance we do whatever we can to get away from that feeling; whether it be to immerse ourselves in a job or an activity, or to pursue our desires, or to express our sexuality in some shape or form, or to control another living being, or even to hide from our pain by sleeping. But what is it that we are really running from? The essence of what we are feeling, however it manifests itself, never seems to go away, yet we seem no closer to understanding the true nature of these feelings.

So let's do just that and get to know the creator of so many of our disabling feelings that leave us lost in the Insanity of Humanity.

The evolution of Pain's Domain

For millions of years during the evolution of life on this planet, the necessary pathways for the expression of pain were developing. This expression, if it was to have any impact, required the development of living creatures that could physically and tangibly interact with their environment. All of these living entities needed some kind of force to guide their functioning and decision making, hence the cooperative relationship between pain and life.

Pain enabled living creatures to quickly identify what factors in their external environment were threats to their survival. The symphony that was created between pain and any living entity became one of the greatest factors in determining which manifestations of life would survive.

Right in front of our eyes we can see the results of this evolutionary process and observe the functioning of the intelligence behind pain. We can see this as we observe so many creatures on their journey of survival all driven by the same force. Although humans and other animals have added on an emotional and intellectual interpretation of pain, I recommend that we don't limit our view of it to this narrow vision that we are personally experiencing. Try to see the grander lateral picture of what pain is. It is important to understand where it has come from, how it is travelling through life, and the effects it is having on the behaviour and functioning of all living creatures.

I am particularly interested in observing pain, because the empire which it has built via the mechanisms of life, has very clearly defined characteristics that we have come to believe are just the normal functioning of all living things. For example, it has become accepted practice in human functioning to use control over other living beings in order to attain desired outcomes.

Control is a behavioural technique for survival, grown out of pain; hence, the two cannot be separated. In other words, as long as there is pain in the nature of how we currently experience it, there will be the need to control. And as long as there is control, there will be emotional repression and cruelty, and as long as there is repression, the cycle of pain will continue.

Pain is creating an expression of itself that ensures the continuance of its own existence. Without the correct awareness or knowledge, our lives will simply become a self-fulfilling prophecy of the images that misunderstood pain creates in our minds.

> And misunderstood pain lives in our minds as fear.

The Pain - Human Combo Deal

If pain is to be looked at as an energy force and arguably a form of intelligence, then it is certainly very patient. The necessary ingredients that pain needed to connect to and expose its power were not served up by life quickly! This is something that most people forget; that is, the massive amount of time and rearrangement of matter that has transpired for the situation that we are experiencing today to exist. Particularly in western society where we are caught up in such an obsessive, self-indulgent and quick-fix mentality that we are not spending the time to understand the power and depth of the forces that are guiding our existence.

Why?

Because of the pain we feel. The greater the pain the more desperate we become. So it is essential that we stop running away from pain and sit in it long enough to understand it, otherwise it will continue to control and distort our existence.

For the expression of pain to have any great and noticeable impact on life, an entity that had high levels of intelligence, mobility and dexterity was necessary for the development of a powerful relationship. After many years of experimentation nature certainly supplied the perfect creation to match these qualities – human beings.

Since our appearance on this planet, we have developed to become one of the most powerful influencing entities on Earth. Pain has established itself as the key guiding force for our decision-making. In fact, I would suggest that pain was a great influence in the development of the human mind. Given the power we have as a species and given that it is pain that is consuming our lives, what sort of world do you think we are creating?

One that represents pain!

It is interesting to consider that pain could take control of our lives, to the point where our behaviour becomes highly predictable; particularly in light of the fact that most people believe they have freedom of choice.

Predictability is necessary for the purpose of maintaining control.

Because of the predictable characteristics that pain as a system of guidance creates, it has been able to maintain its rule over all living creatures. You can see that we have become victim to this system of pain because of our desperate need for predictability in our own lives - a perfect trap but not impenetrable.

This is where things now get fascinating and very fortunate for us.

The key word that will help free us is *predictable*. Although this quality serves the intelligence behind pain perfectly, it does mean that the behaviour it creates in all living creatures can be observed and understood - even within the complex functioning of the human mind. This behaviour is actually a system of information, a secret hidden code. When seen in its entirety beyond the superficial layers of our existence, it actually holds the key to the next phase of our journey. Pain is embodied with a wealth of wisdom that can teach us to live beyond our existing, primitive and reactive modes of functioning.

So all we need is an observer that can exist in the midst of pain. This is a necessary characteristic; otherwise, the observer will only be viewing through a narrow window of surveillance. If the observer were not within the Pain Zone, the surveillance would lead to nothing but an interesting notation of facts.

Fortunately there is the perfect entity for this task just waiting to be stirred from its slumber – and that is the essence of the energy that is us!

Conscious Energy is able to observe the mind, separate from the mind and at the same time exist within the mind. Yet as things stand we are so lost in the world of pain that we think this is our world, as opposed to a world that we are in - a world that holds within it a journey into a new realm of existence.

It would appear that although Conscious Energy already exists within the Pain Zone, waking it up to serve its purpose in this Universe is not as simple as we would like it to be. The illusion that pain has created is not as easy to see through as people might think.

The entry point of Conscious Energy

Let's take another step backwards into the evolution of the development of life and its ally pain.

The various prototypes and working models of *the brain* continued to evolve until nature created a brain that could potentially and adequately function as a representative of life itself.

Pain's Domain

Our human-like ancestors, who did not survive, used pain to create some sense of order to life so they could prioritise, categorise and separate one thing from the other. The limitation to this process was that it only stimulated very basic thinking. In this mode the mind became single-mindedly focused on how to survive. Once a reasonable sense of survival was achieved there was no need to explore beyond that – hence they were primarily living in the now. So pain alone was not enough to create the insatiable desires we see in humans today and the suffering they produce.

It is a commonly held notion that technological advancement and human mastery over the physical realm remained reasonably stagnant for over one million years, until a sudden change occurred.

The following is a proposition for the sake of exploration and to increase awareness by expanding our vision of life. I would suggest that a transformation happened; a new ingredient emerged on the stage of life, something that when combined with pain would enhance the ability of an intelligent creature to explore the external environment. The advent of this new force created a greater need for control in order to fulfil the mind's new questioning ability and higher level of imagination. With this increased intelligence and creativity also came more fear, owing to a more complex network of thought growing in the human mind. So this new ingredient also had to be something that not only created a new level of functioning for the mind, but also something that could be controlled and hence manage fear.

This new chemistry of brain functioning that entered the arena of life created an evolutionary shift of great magnitude; opening the realms of possibility to either a potentially dangerous, or a potentially life saving formula.

I strongly suggest that this new ingredient was Conscious Energy. Conscious Energy combined with human thought allowed for the questioning of not just one's existence, but also the evaluation of which pathway to walk. So, the human mind became aware that it had Conscious Energy inside it, which created the beginning of awareness - albeit at a relatively unevolved state. This sparked a noticeable turning point for our human ancestors to break free from their existing mode of functioning. Their desire to explore beyond immediate survival became an additional and powerful driving force. They were now able to look into the future and question the nature of their existence.

> **This new ability to question life would have also led to the beginning of the questioning of who and what they were - the beginning of The Ego.**

If we were to measure evolutionary success by the fact that we actually exist today, then the powerful mixture of pain and Conscious Energy within the human mind was definitely an incredible and successful combination. However, if we look at where this journey has taken us to this very point in time, then we could easily say that if we are to use suffering as a guide, this combination is no longer working for us.

So, either we need a new ingredient, or we need to shift the dynamic somehow - or both.

Even if Conscious Energy has an element of awareness attached, without a powerful injection of integrity and compassion, the kill or be killed mentality that pervades the planet today will persist. Integrity and compassion are not just concepts, they actually exist, yet we can see this is not something we have yet learnt how to embrace.

Like pain, see Conscious Energy as a force that is totally separate from, but having the ability to interact with the physical realm via the conceptual realm. When this invisible energy found its way into the structures of living entities, it would have injected a greater level of exploratory thinking than had ever been experienced before by a living being. From a human perspective, it would have greatly enhanced the ability to question one's own existence, and this would have stimulated the need to find the appropriate answers. This I would propose was the beginning of the true development of the powerful relationship between the human mind and pain. The need to control and understand the external world was now the focus of the mind's attention.

The question you may be asking now is; why, if Conscious Energy is within the human mind, do we continue down a pathway of control and destruction?

Based on what can be witnessed in today's world, I would suggest as a plausible theory, that Conscious Energy at this point was just that - energy! It had not transformed completely into Conscious Awareness. It had entered, or was created within the conceptual realm for the first time, and it either lost or had no sense of awareness of what it actually was, or more accurately, where it was. Inevitably during this phase of confusion it was taken over by pain and the power of the Problem-Solving Mind.

So it was not long before Conscious Energy believed it was the mind and all that it perceived, and it joined in on the journey of discovery via the processes of controlling the external world. A world which it erroneously believed was now separate from it, as opposed to realising that it was actually within it, and therefore potentially able to influence the creation of it. And when I say within it, remember that we are not in the world in the way the movie of our life plays out. We are inside an intangible experience using our body to create the human journey. And don't jump to the conclusion that where we actually reside is inside the mind, but rather the minds creation, its cyber world of thoughts, feelings and imagery.

Whether this is true or not, really does not matter, because all we need to understand is that we are currently living inside a conceptual version of a physical and psychological structure, and that we are being guided by forces that inevitably control our existence. The intelligence behind the mechanisms of pain works in harmony with these structures as it manipulates Conscious Energy to intertwine all of these aspects of life.

A formidable team and we are right in the middle of it!

So although Conscious Energy is a beautiful and pure force in itself, it has the potential (without appropriate awareness, integrity and compassion) to create great harm and damage to everything around us and to ourselves.

> **The brain is being utilised as a tool and that tool is housed inside the vehicle that we identify as being a human, as being us.**

But we are not a human being; we are Conscious Energy inside a human-being. And this is a very important concept to grasp in the process of developing appropriate awareness.

Driving school

The human brain is being used as an instrument to play out a certain version of life. This observation leads us to see that any mechanism of functioning is simply a representative of what is actually guiding it. For example, if it is being guided by something akin to what we would define as evil, then evil is what it shall create. So ideally we need to learn how to transform our awareness of what we are, and where we are, to the point where we can drive this incredible piece of machinery with integrity. But this will never happen until we learn to decode the hidden message within the sensation of pain – as this is how one can transform Conscious Energy into Conscious Awareness and then into Conscious Awareness with all encompassing compassion and integrity. This then opens up portals to embrace the infinite nature of our potential to think and explore, which defies the minds attempts to see life as a problem in a finite sense. Now we are living in the realm of possibilities and our integrity guides our actions that arise from such exploration, hence the need to control disappears.

In this sense I would like you to look at this book as the manual to understanding the mechanics of the human mind and how to drive this vehicle effectively. The extra advantage of understanding the information that I am sharing is that you will be able to fix the vehicle every time it breaks down.

To try and create some inspiration, look at the human mind as an incredibly sophisticated spaceship that has the ability to travel through space and time, thus giving you the opportunity to experience, explore and understand all that you encounter. The more you develop the skills for handling this spaceship the greater the adventure that will be waiting for you. However, without awareness of the forces guiding your thoughts, this will never happen.

Skipping classes

It would appear that either no one turned up to school to understand how to drive this vehicle, or there has been no one to teach us how to use it in the first place. The evidence would certainly point to the latter. Despite the ongoing development of our mastery over the physical realm, humanity is still emotionally experiencing life at similar level, albeit more complex, as their primitive ancestors - we just have bigger and more elaborate toys to play with!

The amazing advances in technology simply create the illusion that we are more advanced. But we are not, as true advancement is evidenced in pain's ability to manipulate us. The majority of us who utilise technology have little understanding of it, or of the forces that created it, and we are therefore unwittingly at the mercy of it.

Traditionally we have used the knowledge we have acquired in an attempt to try and increase our ability to control what we see.

And this very behaviour is the illusion of control as it is the pathways of pain that are creating the desire and need for control in the first place. We are caught in a world where we are chasing a notion of hope and happiness to escape the sensation of pain. Fear within the human mind is increasing, because we are becoming more and more confused as to how to attain the notion of happiness that we think is real. It really is an amazing thing once you see it, as you can sit in awe over the blinding simplicity of what we have somehow missed on our insane and painful journey. We have become so obsessed with running from our pain that we have literally not been able to see what was right in front of us all along. It does not matter how fast we run or even where we hide, pain follows us everywhere we go – so we may as well stop and have a closer look at what it really is.

Blind in the midst of our own intelligence

We, as supposedly advanced, intelligent and aware beings, are oblivious as to what forces are primarily guiding us, hence the continuing journey that we are witnessing into the Insanity of Humanity. As long as we continue to think we are in control, then pain will continue to be the master of our domain.

So it would be reasonable to propose that it is not our domain at all, it is in fact Pain's Domain.

When you think about it, the mastery behind how this system of functioning works is truly deserving of the control that it maintains over us.

The unfolding of the intelligence behind all of this doesn't stop here. Pain and the fear that it produces have also been the key elements guiding the creation of our beliefs. So here we are letting our beliefs guide the journey of our lives when the very thing that is destroying us, that is pain, created these beliefs. You, as Conscious Energy, barely get the chance to even cope with the daily functioning of the emotional roller coaster that living in a belief structure creates, let alone come to some awareness of where you are so you can actually understand what is going on. This is however, the perfect situation for keeping us psychologically trapped in a world where we think that we need to be in control, while at the same time, we can't understand why we cannot maintain this control.

So how do you think we as a species have responded to this ever-present dilemma? We continue to try and get more control of course.

This is where the insanity of human behaviour becomes very obvious. Despite thousands of years of human evolution and the possibility to pass wisdom on from one generation to another, we continue to raise our levels of control to solve this *perceived problem* - and so on we go, caught in a loop of unsolvable disturbance.

When I look at this picture that I am presenting I see one of the greatest masterpieces that I have ever had the privilege to witness. It is truly ingenious - and it works! Pain combined with Conscious Energy within the human mind creates the notion that life is a problem that needs solving. However, in reality there is no such thing as a problem. A problem is just a perceptual notion that is created when your mind has decided that life is not heading the way it wants it to, which is nearly always!

Of course this is just a lure that pain creates to ensure that this is where our attention stays focussed. Perceiving something to be a problem doesn't change what is.

As long as you see life as something that it is not, you will never actually see life!

It would appear to me, that from the position where pain is sitting, everything is going to plan and almost nobody seems to be aware of it. People in general are fighting for their fear and therefore the justification of increasing levels of control. But fear is not as powerful as you might think; it is just a sensation that travels down the perceptual pathways created by pain. Yet all of humanity is enforcing their fear on the world, and in the process justifying the cruelty and destruction that is manifesting in their behaviour.

Can you see the insanity in this?

> **Pain is the common link between all of us and hence we are creating a world that represents this.**

There can be only one winner in all of this and it will not be us – irrespective of what beliefs we are holding onto in order to justify our insanity.

It has been a long journey for the intelligence behind pain to get to the point where it could guide and influence the processes of a sophisticated piece of machinery such as a human being. Because of our high levels of brain-power and varied physical abilities, the potential of what we are capable of doing is enormous; so our ability to create the obliteration of all life on this planet is colossal.

We have supposedly taken full control over this planet and it is pain that drives all of our decisions whether we know it or not. The false notion that pervades the ever-present human-centred attitude that we see in today's world, is that human intelligence has taken control over the planet. However, I present to you the idea that it is in fact the intelligence behind the functioning of pain that has control over us.

> **A human being, like all of life, is nothing more than a manifestation of the energy that guides it.**

If what I am presenting to you seems in any way illogical, absurd, or maybe something that belongs in the realm of science fiction, then ask yourself: if we are in control of our existence, and if we are as genuinely intelligent and aware as we like to think, then why are we continuing towards the obvious and predictable annihilation of our own species?

Also, why would any individual person live in any state of psychological discomfort if they had a choice to do otherwise?

And more importantly:

> **Why would we justify the murder of other living creatures for our own pleasure, and at the same time expect to feel good about ourselves?**

Given how *intelligent* we are, surely if pain was just something that we were experiencing in response to an unpleasant stimulus, would it not therefore be quite straightforward to rise above it, hence allowing wisdom to be the guiding force on our journey?

Do not underestimate what we are witnessing on our planet; the truth is right in front of us to see, but we will first need to understand the forces that are disallowing us from accepting and acting on this information.

If you would like a little clue at this point, then observe the nature of any resistance that you may be feeling in response to what I am presenting. This is the energy that created the beliefs that you feel the need to defend - an energy which is driving all of humanity towards darkness. Once we have been drawn into this place of existence we will never be able to return to fulfil the potential to live the consciously evolved existence that awaits us today – unless we stop and see the light now!

> **Pain, without us waking up, will create nothing but a world of darkness as it cannot exist in the light for very long.**

The light that is our saviour is life unedited in its purest and uncorrupted form – and this light is in fact compassion expanded beyond perception. And it is Consciousness in a state of awareness with integrity that can allow this truth to enter our minds. But we never see this light because our beliefs are purpose-built by the Problem-Solving Mind to obstruct it from our view.

Everything that we see, witness and experience is another clue for us to put the pieces of the puzzle together. But we first need to stop looking at everything from the perspective of being a human being. Otherwise we will keep responding to life in a primitive survival based mode, where pain will be our ever-present guide that will take us to our death.

Embodied in the knowing that lies within these observations is our chance as a species to find true spiritual freedom and the possibility to redirect our life out of the Insanity of Humanity.

Interestingly, pain has brought us to this point in time, disguising the possibility to observe and understand ourselves, and now it is supplying us with unavoidable reasons to rise above it.

PHASE THREE

Is pain the key to our freedom?

The mechanisms of pain

One of the key and founding forces in the development of human behaviour is that we are programmed to remove ourselves from anything that causes pain – whatever the source. Most important for the purposes of this discussion is the fact that the experience of pain includes a cognitive and emotional component of fear, anxiety, and a powerful feeling of unpleasantness. Note, as things currently stand, we think that the feelings that are part of, connected to, or associated with pain, are only those that consist of any sensation ranging from mild discomfort through to deep disturbance. Opposed to this is the understanding that the entirety of our experience of life is in fact an expression of pain.

Once we receive a stimulus that triggers any of the sensations that we perceive to be from the pain family, the Problem-Solving Mind will focus its attention on this specific aspect of its experiential reality in an attempt to ascertain the true nature of the stimulus. It will then decide where to position this experience in its structure and put in place protective measures for the future. Pain is then recorded in the mind as a memory that becomes part of our beliefs. This psychological recording can be aroused into action by any new stimulus that is somehow associated with the original experience. During this process, depending on the severity of how the pain is felt, the Problem-Solving Mind has the ability to temporarily filter out all other information received from life that is not directly pertaining to the issue at hand.

So given that we seem so interested in using pain as a barometer in our decision making, it is very important to clearly understand that pain is not only felt in direct response to actual physical damage, but by any thought pathways that convincingly represent the concept of a physical threat, or a threat to our well being in general.

If you really would like to open your mind, then embrace the reality that any emotion without awareness embodied in it, is in fact an expression of pain. We are obsessed with protecting ourselves from pain, yet at the same time we cannot make decisions without it.

So it is not hard to imagine the dilemma this presents to our minds. Particularly when we consider that we are unaware, owing to the process of clever programs, that our whole experience is currently an expression of pain.

Is it all just a dream?

While attached to the world of pain we can never really find any true sense of comfort in our existence, hence we are stuck in the mode of problem-solving. So in an attempt to resolve this dilemma, the Problem-Solving Mind utilises the process of dreaming. In a dream state we desperately try to understand our strained comprehension of life within the realms of the pain that we are experiencing. This is reflected in the fact that more often than not, dreams have a powerful feeling of discomposure. The dream state is also a perfect example of how pain can be felt when there is no external stimulus whatsoever, other than our own thinking. If we can bring this awareness of the power of our dream states and the emotions that they can create to the forefront of our minds, then I suggest that it is time to start asking ourselves what is real and what is not, in a more open-minded and lateral sense.

If you can accept the notion that all is not as it seems, then I would also like you to accept that we all have the latent ability to alter our sensitivity to pain and the suffering that is experienced in association with it - whether it is on a physical or emotional level. Of greatest concern for the discussions in this book, is how the Problem-Solving Mind experiences, creates and uses pain from a cognitive and emotional point of view.

Pain has led us into the Insanity of Humanity and now we can use it to lead us out!

The potential purpose of pain

Relative to life as a human being, pain can be seen as the consequence of our minds' interpretation of stimuli relative to our belief structure and programmes. It is used as a gauge and a fuel source to create an ongoing web of interconnected cognitive patterns of thought in order to produce behavioural responses for the purpose of survival.

Without our minds, pain would have no purpose in the journey towards higher consciousness and therefore could not be utilised. However, without us (Conscious Energy), the mind would be a manifestation of pain in pure isolation.

Pain in the human brain can be felt over something that is just a notion in our head. At this point it is important to point out that no pain, and therefore no emotion, should be disregarded; whether it is experienced because of a real threat in the physical sense, or a perceived threat of something that might happen in the future, or over something we falsely believe is happening now. Because pain is pain and either we are experiencing it or we're not. Never ignore it. All pain is real and it can all be utilised for our journey. The key is to understand what it is telling us, or more importantly, let it lead us to what it is that we do not currently understand.

To understand pain it is essential to embrace all of our emotions!

If we are aware of the relationship between pain and our Problem-Solving Mind, then we have the ability to change the current purpose of pain from one of control, through the process of creating fear, to a purpose whereby pain is used to guide us to the next phase of human evolution - a phase where the deeper underlying message embodied in pain can be utilised. This message is that wisdom can be acquired when the human mind and Conscious Energy develop an intelligent and healthy alliance. This new purpose can only be found through the process of awareness and freedom of emotional expression. This will require us to stop compartmentalising, segregating and controlling which emotions we allow ourselves to feel.

> To go on an expansive journey into a state of higher consciousness requires feeling everything - not just what you want to feel.

A merger of intellectual systems

Without pain human beings may not have survived to this point, as the mind would not have known how to distinguish one thing from another in its decision-making processes. So from that point of view we could easily argue that pain is our ally and therefore our friend. In fact it would not be difficult to be convinced that it is actually quite a symbiotic relationship. However, pain appears to have the ability to get into the systems of life and use it for its own purpose. Metaphorically speaking, if pain was to be thought of as an alien life form, it is now using us to continue the building of a life which represents the essence of its existence, and that essence would appear to be all about fear, control and destruction.

Pain, if seen as a separate form of intelligence, helps us to understand it. However we look at it, it represents a system of life, and all systems are either created by or have some form of advanced intellectual process behind the flow and development of their existence.

Please note: although I am separating the different factors as a learning aid; always remember that all aspects of life and all systems of intelligence are interconnected, and hence part of the one overall journey, of the one overall truth.

A mergence of darkness and light

Pain and Conscious Energy do have one thing in common though. They are both forms of intelligence and both require other forms of life to continue the expression and development of their existence. What we are currently witnessing within the human mind is simply the struggle between these two types of energy - we have labelled this dichotomy as the battle between good and evil. It is possible not to see either types of energy as right or wrong, or good or evil, but to simply become aware of this reality. Within this awareness we can assist the Problem-Solving Mind in decoding these two forms of intelligence, bringing forth an understanding of pain and us into this reality. Rather than either of the two being expelled, there could be a joining of both to create a unified force. This is the larger, more elaborate picture of life that I have painted, however for the purpose of your existence now, I will focus on the reality of these energies and how we can get the process of awareness started. This will give our mind a chance to deal with the forces that life has presented it with - to give us a chance to deal with and understand our emotions.

Mercy please!

When we feel that to be alive is a painful experience, we will tend to get angry and blame the circumstances surrounding us for how we feel, or for what we feel we are being subjected to. It feels appropriate to blame the external world because we feel like we are at the mercy of it, or at the very least, like we're at the mercy of something other than us. And we are, but it is not the external world that we are at the mercy of . . .

> We are experiencing the painful and confusing roller coaster ride of life without unleashed compassion and awareness.

So if we're looking for mercy, we should give up this idea immediately, as this is just a notion created by pain and fear. The intelligence behind pain will certainly never have mercy on us. There is not necessarily malicious intent behind this process, but I would suggest that it would be wise for us to recognise its existence. So our only hope of survival is to wake up to the reality of our existence, to the reality that we are Conscious Energy functioning inside the human mind.

Also note at this point that although the essence of us is Conscious Energy, we too are able to experience ourselves via the thinking processes of our minds. And although this vision is currently quite distorted, the truth of what we are is embodied within our minds.

Pain is like a virus

A virus does not show any of the properties attributed to living systems, but when a virus particle enters a living cell, it is able to reproduce thousands of copies of itself. A virus is thus a replicating molecular unit that is dependent upon living cells to provide the energy and molecular machinery necessary for its own duplication.

If left unchecked pain spreads like a virus corrupting the whole system of functioning in our minds. Just as we can't change the fact that a virus has entered our system, neither can we change the fact that pain has entered our minds. However, we can change how we deal with it. So, like the way our immune system becomes stronger after we survive the onslaught of a virus, so does our mind develop more structural integrity and wisdom once we face and deal with the corruption that pain can, or has caused in our brains.

PHASE THREE

Detoxifying your mind

The human mind's job is to deal with the external world and the information that it presents. This clever piece of programming is able to hold up a multitude of social masks. These masks are created to disguise the confusing 'behind the scenes' processes of analysing and sorting the information of life - information that it is constantly collecting and filtering. These social masks that tend to limit our life, are an edited and limited version of us. When we believe that our social masks are us, we deny ourselves the possibility to cleanse the systems of our minds - a necessary process for us to see life clearly and therefore interpret it accurately. When the cleansing process is active, all emotional experiences are embraced. In this mode we would not take life's experiences personally and so any pain that may be associated with this experience is removed and replaced with wisdom. In this instance we are still experiencing life via our emotions, but the difference is that they are injected with awareness. And given that pain is the lifeblood of life, then it is easy to see that this is where our awareness needs to reside.

When the cleansing process is not active, the mind is absorbing every experience and soaking up misunderstood pain as a necessary ingredient in its functioning - filtering out the information that is necessary for the building of wisdom. Pain is the minds means of support, and the nature of the minds functioning dictates that it takes everything personally, as it is through this process that it creates its sense of self and its sense of place in the world.

When the pain that the mind is so heavily reliant upon is not detoxified, it becomes the poison that corrupts our existence; it becomes a force in its own right. In this instance the mind can sense that it is experiencing levels of pain that is making its own functioning quite difficult and confusing. So the minds response is to get the social masks working even harder at their job of protection. Therefore it increases the screening process, whereby we end up experiencing life from an even narrower framework. It knows no other way to solve this apparent problem, and whether it realises this or not, the mind is actually driving itself towards its ultimate demise.

Without our Conscious Awareness to channel in the unedited version of life, the mind becomes addicted to pain while at the same time addicted to wanting to feel good. This is a very disturbing and soul destroying cycle of functioning that we get caught in as we proceed to collect pain as a source of power. This process is the underlying reality behind all human addictions.

> So as things stand for all of us, our whole life is a form of addiction to something . . .
>
> An addiction to our life story!

To clarify - the cleansing process is only active when our Conscious Energy is in a state of complete and expansive compassion and awareness. Then we are no longer addicted to anything.

The reservoir of pain

As our life progresses, if we do not have the cleansing process in place, we run the risk of accumulating our painful experiences, effectively forming a reservoir in which to store them. This reservoir is hidden in different parts of our life story, which are all connected to form one reality - the one that we currently exist in.

When the next painful experience arises, we will not just experience pain relevant to that situation, we will potentially draw on specific parts of, or sometimes the entire reservoir of pain, and use this to fuel our chosen action in response to the perceived threat. At the very least, we will draw on any pain from the reservoir which is attached to a memory of an experience that is somehow associated to the one we are experiencing now.

Whatever the scenario, our reactions to life will be exaggerated and inappropriate relative to the actual stimulus.

Once the stimulus or perceived threat has been removed, at least in a physical and immediate sense, we retreat back into the deep confines of our mind and remain in a permanent state of alertness - ranging from the sensation of very subtle discomfort or agitation, through to quite extreme anxiety or panic attacks.

Although we may no longer be directly responding in a fight or flight manner, these mechanisms are still active and ready for action. As each new experience of pain is absorbed, the boundaries of the reservoir increase in structural strength and more than likely in volume too - hence it has become more powerful and therefore more capable of aiding in higher levels of destructive behaviour than before.

As our pain increases in quantity, our life story contains us in an increasingly stressful reality, as its restrictive boundaries get stretched to their limits.

When our reservoir of pain becomes very large and dominant as one of our behavioural influences, it has the potential to create a powerful and distorted anger or sadness response of equivalent strength. In these moments we feel supercharged with energy, as we have our pain reservoir to resource our defensive reactions to life. Our responses, when our mind is in this mode, are extremely illogical, improper and many degrees of separation from the truth. However, although our behaviour is no longer creating a journey for us of any reasonable substance, it feels extremely real as if it is the truth. In this sense, pain can become a dangerously addictive energy as it gives us a false sense of power and a false sense of being in control. I assure you, these surges of power are not empowerment, as they are functioning through a system without any structural integrity.

Is pain the key to our freedom?

High levels of pain lead us to believe that we must defend our life story in order to maintain it, under the false belief that we are the story!

The beast!

If our mind perceives a stimulus to be a significantly large threat to its status quo, it will unite and undergo a metamorphosis into a programmed rage monster. This beast will have its full intent on either retreating from, or destroying any perceived threat in its path. When this program is active, a person is virtually disconnected from the majority of their psychological and spiritual network of human functioning. Then they are travelling down a potentially dangerous and destructive pathway with an extremely narrow focus. This program's focus is immediate survival – created by the Problem-Solving Mind. Every single one of us has the potential, in the right circumstances, to bring this program to life. It is built to destroy or remove itself from anything that stands in the way between it and its notion of survival. I am not just referring to survival in terms of running away, for example, from a dangerous predator or any other obvious physical threat. I am referring to the process by which a person feels the need to protect the world of their life story and all of the key elements in it.

Irrespective of the stimulus, for this program to appear means that a person's beliefs were already holding on to a tenuous thread of meaning.

When we are trapped in this place of extreme defence, the Problem-Solving Mind sees its perceived threat as far more than just a problem that needs solving. It is not functioning under a false notion either, for to remove its home, its network of intertwined beliefs, would lead to its demise and it knows this. Even though an outsider who is observing someone in this state may describe this person's behaviour as irrational, ridiculous and even insane relative to his or her own belief structure, to the mind of the person experiencing it, it is very real. It cannot take the risk of being destroyed, and therefore its normal mode of functioning (whereby it uses the social masks for dealing with perceived problems) would be totally inadequate. People in this state of functioning are extremely dangerous to anything or anyone that stands between the notion of where they are and where they feel they need to be to feel safe.

A person can always tell when someone has slipped into this mode, as his or her demeanour changes dramatically, their energy becomes focused and you will sense an intensity of boiling rage under the surface of their social mask. This is easily identified when you look into their eyes. In this mode the person has fully tapped into their reservoir of pain and they are no longer reasonable, rational or interested in anything other than their own survival. Hence the potential for corruption is at its highest level and integrity is most certainly absent.

These moments of unprotected pain expose the truth of what underlies all of our thinking.

This is the energy we need to observe more honestly and stop being in denial of its existence. This is why it is so easy to take a person, once exposed to the appropriate triggers, from a place of apparent confidence to a place of great disturbance.

The disturbance is what we need to expose, understand and stop protecting!

Depending on the size of a person's reservoir of pain and depending on the structural integrity of their beliefs, it will vary how easily such a person can be triggered into that mode. Also, if a person goes there regularly it will become an addictive and soul-destroying place of existence. Interestingly in this situation, a person's behaviour does not always instantly appear as obvious rage. Often they will become very quiet initially as they are desperately trying to analyse their environment to ascertain the necessary path of survival. If they are unable to get back to a safe haven quickly enough, their boiling undercurrent quickly turns into more obvious signs of rage and potentially they will become physically violent to themselves or others.

As time progresses and these dangerous programs are allowed to stay living within the confines of our minds, the reservoir of pain will progressively grow into a conceptual creature with greater levels of distorted pain and anger attached to its existence.

The power of pain that we have become so heavily reliant on, is in fact the power that is draining our lives.

This power is only accessible for brief defined periods of time. Once the moment of rage or despair has dissipated and we are disconnected from the reservoir, we are left feeling weak, fatigued and almost pathetic in comparison to the energy that was so briefly ours.

Extreme expressions of happiness are connected to the same process!

This is why it is such an addictive way of functioning. The mind once removed from this powerful energy becomes confused as it tries to scramble and recreate some semblance of meaning in its existence – it feels out of control!

The notion of control is the mind's constant goal and an erroneously identified safe haven; an asylum that it thinks will protect it from the dangers that prowl in its world.

This process I have just described comes and goes repeatedly throughout the functioning of our daily lives; and it is often dependent on how much we are resisting the events of the day.

So it does not always continue to grow into a fully formed beast, but the potential for it is always alive and well.

Always remember, wherever we are sitting on the emotional spectrum, all feelings are representatives of pain until we become Consciously Aware and complete in our expression of compassion. This is something most people do not realise, so we stay trapped in the Construct - our life story.

Sharing the rage behind our beliefs

It is important to also become aware of how these modes of functioning can potentially create great force when people have their pain ignited simultaneously, in a frenzy of power and rage. This is an example of the Insanity of Humanity in all its glory.

We do not have to watch the news on television for too many nights in a row before we will get the chance to witness this kind of behaviour somewhere in the world. Rage and fury can spread very quickly and rapidly in this kind of situation, because any sense of individual responsibility that society had placed on them very quickly disappears. In this instance people justify their behaviour underneath the blanket of the shared story of pain. It is extraordinary what we are all capable of doing in this mode of functioning. Once again the truth that underlies our behaviour is exposed.

Call 911 we have an emergency!

Stop and have an honest look at the mechanisms of our minds, and their connection to pain within us and other individuals that we interact with on the journey of our life. If we do not see the process that we have become subconsciously connected to, we will ultimately create the demise of what we have falsely identified with as our existence.

Is pain the key to our freedom?

Every time we have a powerful pain-based experience our beliefs get shaken at their foundations, until eventually the mind can no longer maintain and repair its construct of thought any more. If we were to experience this scenario, we would at the point when our beliefs had finally become insubstantial in our mind, relinquish the survival process of blaming and trying to control the external environment. The Problem-Solving Mind would then turn its attention elsewhere and abandon its alliance with all of its (our) social masks. Quickly realising that it has nowhere else to direct its need to be in control, the mind would then attack its own creations, as it has now identified the artificial versions of us as the problems that need solving. It finds only one answer to this incredibly painful experience, and that is extermination. Once we have been pushed to this point our behaviour will become desperately erratic, irrational and highly destructive to ourselves and anybody around us - now we genuinely have an emergency on our hands, as depression and anxiety will manifest in our daily functioning.

When the mind gets to the point of meltdown, this can either be our opportunity to step back and see the true nature of the Problem-Solving Mind while it is weak and confused, or it will lead to us being attached to a mental breakdown, suicide, or the destruction of other living things.

To summarise...

Pain effects the expression of all aspects of life including our personality, how our learning is formed, our sexuality, our dreams and desires, our concepts of success, happiness, love - everything. It is the fuel that flows through the pathways of The Problem-Solving Mind and hence the Construct in which we are housed.

This is why it is essential to stop immediately when it's recognised that pain and the mind are driving our lives via our Conscious Energy. Otherwise, every thought and corresponding feeling we have will be corrupted by the pain, and this is a continuous building process that has no structural integrity. Thoughts and feelings just keep playing off each other in manipulated cycles of insanity as they create the life that we are currently experiencing.

Remember, this whole process that I am exploring throughout the book is simply to take us to a place where we can be aware. Awareness is one of the most powerful things that we will ever create; so do not underestimate the effectiveness of it. We just need to know what to be aware of. At this point be aware that we may still be experiencing life from a limited phase of consciousness; meaning that the energy that is us has not fully woken up to its existence beyond all that it is experiencing.

Further down the awareness pathway it is possible to eventually create a mind that has no life story as such. Instead we can learn how to allow all information to sit in what effectively could be thought of as a 'resource centre' - this is life unedited - rather than the one corrupted by pain and the fear it creates.

If we are fully content with our current experiential reality then there is no need to change. But know that if we wake up completely, our current alliance to pain will change, as pain cannot maintain its control while the light of awareness is on it. So if we are not content with our lives, then we should start exploring our feelings, and in the process we will discover that we are actually exploring pain – exploring what it is that is creating everything we feel.

And remember:

> ## Our feelings are not always the truth, but it is through exploring our feelings that we can find the truth.

So it is important that we learn not to act on everything that we feel until we understand what it is that we are feeling.

PHASE FOUR

The Problem-Solving Mind

PHASE FOUR

I know I am alive, well at least I think I am. I fear death and yet strangely fear life at the same time. This leaves me lost in a world trapped between these two concepts that I witness, yet neither do I understand.

The Problem-Solving Mind

What is the Problem-Solving Mind?

The Problem-Solving Mind is what the human brain becomes when it is being guided predominantly by pain and fear. It is the mechanical and analytical aspect of our experiential reality, and it is the architect and creator of our life story.

It is an incredibly sophisticated and highly developed piece of thinking machinery. Within every individual mind, it is steering and uniting all of humanity towards an objective that satisfies its pain-driven desires of control.

Everything the Problem-Solving Mind is experiencing we are experiencing. So when I talk about the Problem-Solving Mind, what I am really talking about is the manner in which we are currently functioning in this world. Every single aspect of our existence that we identify as being us, is a specifically crafted version based on our genetic structure and learning.

So what we are experiencing is not life itself, but simply the information that the Problem-Solving Mind has chosen to present us with. The presentation of this information is able to create a dynamic that we have become so heavily reliant upon existing in, that we have not developed the necessary knowledge or skills to know otherwise.

It has created an artificial version of us and life that is so convincing that we actually believe it is real. The most intriguing part is that we are unaware that this is happening, and this is where the truth behind this illusion lies. That is, for this dynamic to be effective, it requires the essence of Conscious Energy to remain in a state where we are effectively asleep. Probably a more accurate analogy would be to imagine that we are trapped somewhere between a conscious and an unconscious state.

There was a time when life was comparatively harsh, cruel and unforgiving for our 'primitive' human ancestors. The concept of fairness was non-existent, for if they were to have indulged in such nonsensical notions they simply would not have survived. It would have been essential that they focused their attention directly on what was necessary to exist in an extremely competitive environment.

Our human ancestors were without question neither the strongest, fastest nor most agile creatures on the planet; in fact, as far as physical prowess is concerned they were functioning with quite a disadvantage. Despite these apparent disadvantages in strength, agility and speed, somehow human beings managed to survive whereby their dominance as a collective species reigns supreme to this day.

So how did we do it? We certainly had great dexterity with our hands. But this was not enough. We needed something else.

We needed the Problem-Solving Mind!

No other species on the planet could even come close to competing with us in our ability to solve problems.

This ability is this key functioning aspect of the human mind that has allowed our ancestors to have survived the most challenging and treacherous of journeys. Allowing us to arrive at the point in time in which we exist today.

Our ancestors would have had to deal with situations that required them to change their whole concept of where and how they could maintain the basic necessities for the continuance of their lives - way beyond any of the triviality that we are so obsessed with in the modern world.

Quite impressive when you really think about it - we are truly an amazing species, surviving against all odds. Not just against the challenges that would have been presented by other species, but also in our ability to adapt to the most extreme of environmental conditions.

The Problem-Solving Mind

Our mastery of problem-solving has ensured our success on our journey from caveman to modern human.

If one was to accumulate all of the thinking power and effort that has been created and expended throughout the journey of the human species, then it would be reasonable to propose that we have certainly earned our position of domination. From this point of view, you can also see how this incredible amount of energy has had a dramatic influence on the shaping of the planet, our minds, the way we think and the civilisations we live in today.

Throughout this journey of survival, the human species has also had the opportunity to utilise its incredible problem-solving and analytical abilities towards developing advanced communication techniques. This has allowed for the acquisition and sharing of information from one individual to another and from one generation to the next.

Our ability to observe and communicate with our Universe is truly amazing!

So you would think that by now our lives would be embodied with incredible levels of wisdom and an understanding of ourselves, and the world in which we live. Potentially, we could all have been harmoniously living together as a species, and jointly sharing the gift of life with the rest of the planet.

But this is far from the truth!

In fact, things appear to be getting worse - we seem to have no ability to effectively use all of this information we have acquired. Everything we create, which is done so with the intent of supposedly making our lives better, seems to be generating the opposite effect.

It would appear that the more we try to control our minds and the environments we interact with, two clearly observable consequences arise:

Firstly, the planet is effectively screaming out in pain as we tear it down and manipulate its existence.

Secondly, the human mind is screaming out with ever increasing levels of fear, suffering and confusion.

> **We are creating a planet that is going to be difficult to live on and a mind that is going to be difficult to live in!**

So what's the deal? How could things possibly be getting worse given the potential brilliance of our minds?

A glitch in the system

Life is not as straightforward as we had hoped. The consequence of being highly advanced problem-solvers is becoming very apparent within the psychological parameters of human functioning.

No matter how much we achieve or attempt to control our environment, we are experiencing more pain and suffering than ever before and it primarily stems from the fact that there is one highly observable but largely overlooked glitch in the functioning of the Problem-Solving Mind.

> **To be a problem-solver you can never be satisfied or you wouldn't bother to solve problems in the first place!**

Think about the consequences that this parameter is having on our lives as we try to find satisfaction, as if it is some place we can arrive and stay at. This apparent eternal realm of dissatisfaction has unwittingly been and is continuing to be shared and transferred via the psychological pathways of human functioning; thus creating a collective consciousness that travels through the very barriers of time, limiting our existence as individuals.

The Problem-Solving Mind

This process leads to ever increasing amounts of pain and suffering, which is reflected by the psychological disorders individuals are experiencing in the world today. As we are permanently trapped in a problem-solving mode, pain increases in intensity as time goes on and this will not stop.

The reason for this is because problem-solving functions in a mode that has a life of its own, so therefore it is an ever growing and evolving entity. As time passes the Problem-Solving Mind's perception of life as a problem increases. The bigger we perceive a problem to be, the more pain it creates when we address it. Then as the pain increases, our vision becomes more blurred and our obsessiveness to control all we see increases; owing to the fear we are experiencing. This is what humanity is currently experiencing as we read this book - unbearable levels of pain. The increasing population of human beings on this planet compounds this; now there are more mental vessels for storing and sharing pain.

But it doesn't stop here . . .

As our perception of the external world being a problem grows, the world that we experience will feel proportionately smaller.

So now we are not just experiencing greater levels of pain, but we are also doing this within a far more restrictive framework of existence. This can be seen in the physical world we are creating, as increasing controls are demanded and implemented in order to create a false notion of security.

How much pain would you like to experience and how small a world would you like to be housed in?

This process I am describing to you is the beginning of the creation of a psychological black hole within our own minds. We are unwittingly creating a force that could eventually hold captive every aspect of our experiential reality.

This psychological black hole is purpose built to contain consciousness.

It has been developing for a long time and its completion is near!

Quite obviously, the techniques of domination and control are not leading to the happiness and security that we thought they would. Humanity is now presented with quite a dilemma. It would be reasonable to propose that we would not knowingly create a pathway towards annihilation. It would also be reasonable to propose that we do not understand the nature and functioning of our own minds, and the forces that are influencing them.

Now think about this:

How could we ever hope that anything we do in our lives could lead to anything that will ever make sense, if we don't even know what we are or where we are? We don't even understand our own emotions - especially when we consider that our emotions create the impulse to act.

As most people are not aware of the life equation that is driving their existence, they blindly continue in their current mode of thinking, desperately hoping that they can problem-solve their way out of the situation in which they find themselves. Or at the very least we hope that our world leaders will find the solutions that we search for. But they too are lost in their world of pain, and are therefore making decisions from a distorted place of existence, whether they admit it or not! The evidence for this is in how they respond to perceived threats. They never outwardly admit that they are lost and confused, but instead profess confidence and stories of future success to justify whatever actions they may invoke. They continue to implement further controls to contain what they do not understand, and they do this without having unleashed their compassion via the expansion of their reality.

The danger of a Problem-Solving Mind without Conscious Awareness is clearly evidenced when any one individual has too much power!

It's not a problem

If we want to continue to be the supposed masters of control, which can only be achieved through the processes of problem-solving, then we are destined to never feel good (to put it gently). The worse we feel the more we become convinced that life is a problem that needs solving.

Do you see humanity's dilemma?

To pull ourselves out of this rather perplexing situation, does this simply mean that we have to improve our ability to decide which aspects of life are problems and which are not?

The answer to this is a resounding no!

It is a matter of understanding that we are trapped in a mind that is built, for survival reasons, to see the entirety of life as a problem. However, although this may sound strange, as part of the intricate mechanisms of this survival process, the Problem-Solving Mind does not think it is seeing all of life as a problem. It thinks it is just seeing certain aspects of life as a problem and therefore comes to the erroneous conclusion that if it controls these identified issues, then there will be no more problems! But, life is always changing, and therefore no matter how much we think we may have gained control over life, these changes quickly become identified as new problems that need solving.

Now we get caught up in the eternal and frustrating illusion of control. That is, we buy into the thinking that if we could just get these new issues under control, then everything will be fine.

Of course, this is a never-ending process.

As our systems of functioning become more complex, and as the information that we share becomes more diluted and confusing, more fear is created. The power of the Problem-Solving Mind is growing exponentially with the increases in our diverse lifestyles.

This is why life so often feels like an insane roller coaster of emotions.

We are spending our lives chasing something that does not exist and our increasing levels of fear are simply giving a false validation to the fact that we should continue to see life as a problem that needs solving.

Life is either a problem, or it isn't.

We can't just see bits and pieces of it as a problem and think that the rest isn't - that is madness!

The above technique of identifying certain aspects of life as a problem blinds us to the truth of what we are experiencing. Our vision becomes very selective and convenient to our fear-based survival objectives. As far as the Problem-Solving Mind is concerned, all of the identified issues it finds unfavourable on the planet today need to be addressed in isolation. Therefore, it will attempt to find solutions in isolation.

The process of building the apparent mess we are today trying to unravel has actually been in development right from the beginning - we just did not see it coming. Now that we have become so heavily reliant upon our existing ways of thinking and the structures they create, the Problem-Solving Mind has us convincingly trapped within its Construct of functioning.

Unless we wake up to the fact that the Problem-Solving Mind planted the seeds that created all of the corruption we see today, then all our efforts to survive will have been in vain.

Really, it's not a problem!

Let's take a closer look at what's going on.

The Problem-Solving Mind finds solutions to life by analysing all of the information that it receives in the now, cross-referencing this information with past knowledge and then projecting a future pathway of thinking for it to travel down. It's in the future that it spends most of its normal functioning. This is why so many people feel stressed and anxious, as they are constantly trying to keep life going the way they want it to.

The Problem-Solving Mind's analytical abilities are primarily focused on trying to create a clear and accurate picture of the entirety of its existence for the purpose of its own survival. These parameters encompass all aspects of life and the external world. This includes the vehicle in which it is housed (our human body), Conscious Energy, our personality, our emotions and all of the information that it receives via its access to our five senses.

Interestingly, it appears to not understand the purpose or meaning of its own existence, in fact it doesn't even know what it is. It has therefore also included itself on its list of things to analyse and understand. The Problem-Solving Mind is trapped in an insatiable and unsolvable quest to understand its own existence and all that it experiences, so it is always scared, insecure and confused, which means we end up trapped in these feelings.

These feelings encompass the following key human qualities that have guaranteed our survival; we are competitive, acquisitive, suspicious, manipulative, controlling and destructive. The underlying reality of our subconscious world functions within the nature of the above mentioned words. The Problem-Solving Mind tries to disguise these qualities by presenting a face of love, compassion, empathy, sympathy, and integrity.

These two divergent realities that exist at the same time within everyone's minds, lead to a distorted, confusing, twisted and dark underworld of thought. We try to protect and hide this world at all costs unless we have the power to expose these qualities without fear of repercussion. The truth of our underlying thoughts can be seen in the behaviour of anyone from corrupt world leaders to a man across the street that kicks his dog when no one is looking.

These realities (in regard to the inner workings of the Problem-Solving Mind) have always been of this nature. However, as civilisation progresses, the outer face of integrity grows in its presentation as it attempts to protect the evolving illness that is manifesting. This process is being accelerated because of the increasing controls being implemented by societies on every individual. In simple terms, the worse things get the more we will try and hide this disturbance by telling ourselves everything is okay. Denial is another rampant quality on planet Earth, but we currently do not understand what it is or how it is created.

Life misreading life

One of the disturbing aspects of our existence is that what we are experiencing is not life itself. However, we think we are and this is the beginning and core root of where the sensations of disturbance start. This erroneous conclusion about the nature of our experiences, leads to the process of enforcing a version of life onto life itself that will never completely fit. Then nothing ever quite makes sense.

> **This is why the Problem-Solving Mind is so concerned with the past and future as it can't seem to find what it is looking for in the now.**

A reasonable and simple analogy would be to say that the Problem-Solving Mind is trying to put a square peg into a round hole. The outcome of this will leave it even more confused than it was in the beginning, because it takes pride in being right and

The Problem-Solving Mind

does not like to concede to being wrong. This makes the Problem-Solving Mind continue to force itself on a situation where there is no fit, under the mistaken belief that eventually it will succeed. Or, it might redirect its attention elsewhere towards a different situation, which will effectively end up creating the same scenario in a different disguise. Either way, the Problem-Solving Mind once again believes that life created the problem, not it, hence justifying its actions and the disastrous consequences they so often create.

Does any of this sound reminiscent of human behaviour? It should, because we are not just living in this world that we see, hear, smell, taste and feel, but also in the conceptual and emotionally dominated world of our minds. And this *place* is predominantly being created in a world of thought beyond our awareness.

The Problem-Solving Mind believes that life is presenting obstacles that cause discomfort. It therefore creates the notion that by rearranging its external environment, it will be able to find the happiness that it is programmed to seek. It just wants life to make sense and has no other way to achieve this, other than to problem-solve all information presented.

Using the above analogy, it thinks that if life (representing the round hole) could change its shape, then everything would be fine. It is very persistent in this belief. However, owing to the fact that it is itself that has misread the situation, its problem-solving pathway is a never-ending and insatiable one. This leads to a permanent state of dissatisfaction and discomfort in the false belief that the answers to finding meaning, security and happiness, lie somewhere in the future in the disguise of another situation to control.

Remember this process of control I am describing is a direct representation of the processes of functioning that we are currently acting out on this planet. It is a mode that justifies the use of force and manipulation to attain a preconceived end result, that either one or many people's Problem-Solving Minds have decided is the superior one.

Untapped creative cyber genius

The Problem-Solving Mind is currently struggling to work out how to harmoniously interact with life, leaving it trapped in a rather simplistic and basic survival mode. However, do not underestimate how brilliant it actually is, and therefore how much potential power it still has to be unleashed.

What it lacks in truth it certainly makes up for in creativity.

Just think about how incredible this is; the Universe has created a mechanism of functioning that is attempting to recreate its own self within a powerful thought-driven, emotional and creative realm. Despite the fact that the Problem-Solving Mind is a few degrees of separation from the truth, it is still reading life with a reasonable degree of accuracy - enough precision to maintain its ability to interact with life, keeping you fooled into thinking that what you are experiencing represents the entirety of what is.

It is important that we do not jump to rapid conclusions as to whether the Problem-Solving Mind is truly effective at its given task or not - and for that matter, we don't want to be too hasty in deciding the exact nature and purpose of its task in this Universe and in our lives. Stay open to the possibility that it may know exactly what it is doing, or at the very least pain knows exactly how to utilise the Problem-Solving Mind.

I would like to reiterate that the Problem-Solving Mind is just one piece in the puzzle of understanding our lives - so please be patient as we work through establishing the foundations for this ongoing exploration.

The Problem-Solving Mind's lack of ability to precisely interpret life, leads it to utilise its extraordinarily imaginative and creative components of functioning. It is bending reality to suit its own

The Problem-Solving Mind

purposes. This is one of the reasons it continues to enforce a distorted version of life onto the world we perceive to be external to us. However, it also leads to a vision of possibilities that would not otherwise have been seen or experienced – it is not limited to what is.

These visions with an appropriate amount of awareness can be used to guide humanity out of its existing state of insanity. I am not negating the abilities of the Problem-Solving Mind, but rather suggesting that we have the ability to change the manner in which it is utilised and use it to aid us in the journey of our existence.

The Problem-Solving Mind is able to project visions of life into your mind, which is responsible for so much of the creative mastery being expressed through avenues like music, art, fiction writing and movie-making.

Even if you don't consider yourself a creative genius, just stop and think about the incredible dreams that you create in your own mind while you are asleep. You are able to produce an internal movie full of characters, dialogue, and emotional responses that are completely interactive, original and dynamic.

So as a species, our creative potential is enormous.

But it is rarely unleashed, because it is currently being utilised by the Problem-Solving Mind for the purpose of creating control – and this effectively equates to maintaining the structural integrity of its life story. It thinks it must first get life under control before it can enjoy the fruits of its own existence. Getting life under control requires emotional repression of oneself and other people.

The Problem-Solving Mind was doing fine when life was much simpler, but the complexities of its own creations are becoming a challenge to manage and understand.

Always remember as you read this book, that you are inside something, and I am trying to help people understand the nature of what that something is. The reason for illustrating this is so you can get a clear understanding of what is happening with your life, so in turn you can learn to sense the experience of being you beyond the restrictive parameters of problem-solving.

Do not underestimate the empowerment that can be created from simply being aware of what I have presented so far.

Think of those moments in your life when there was no internal dialogue in your mind, no stress, no awareness of anything being a problem and in addition, your creativity was powerful and flowing. In these moments you are still experiencing the Problem-Solving Mind, but without editing or controlling the information you are receiving. This opens up all sorts of portals to unleash your potential thinking capabilities by not fearing and needing to protect yourself from life. But if you are not awake and fully aware at these times, you will slip right back into a world of pain and have no idea as to how that happened.

Isn't my perception my truth?

Despite the Problem-Solving Mind's potential brilliance, in the current realm in which it is functioning, it is not completely accurate in its interpretation of life. It is presenting us with a diluted and edited version, compared to what we could potentially be experiencing.

> We are living in a perceptual reality.

You may have heard it said before that there is no reality, just perception. Well this statement is true to a certain point, but not totally accurate in its entirety. This statement is the truth within the realms of the Problem-Solving Mind and all that it creates.

> **To enforce a perception on life as if it is the truth is one of the key parameters for creating the Insanity of Humanity.**

The Problem-Solving Mind

We need to look very closely at what we are currently doing with an open mind, and embrace the idea that we can function beyond our perceptions and therefore our beliefs and our life story.

Consider the following:

Do you enforce your version of life onto other people as if it is the almighty truth, as if your version is 'the' version and the rest of the world should accommodate it? Do you have other people doing the same thing to you? Is your life more about arguments and winning, than compassion and understanding?

Truly consider your answers to these questions before you continue.

Your perception is nothing more than the truth of your perception. It does not encompass the truth of everything, as it symbolises just one very narrow possibility of learning, hence the insanity of trying to enforce it and representing it as something that it is not.

Just see a perception for what it is - a perception!

So let's explore why it is so difficult to let our perceptions stay in a simple state of just being a small amount of interesting knowledge; something that only represents a minute version of the infinite amount of possible information that we could have acquired on the journey of our life experiences.

The Problem-Solving Mind thinks it has access to no other resource for making decisions, other than the knowledge that currently exists within its framework (our perceptions). It is programmed to believe that the information developed through the key and informative years of learning in our childhood, is the bulk of what it needs to know to guide the rest of its existence. It erroneously believes that what it has absorbed is the truth of life, the truth of everything, as opposed to a version that it has created to suit its own needs and purpose.

And we are experiencing life through this constricted corridor of thinking. This is why life always has a restrictive sensation of discomposure, and why it is so hard to openly express what we feel within such a confined space. This is a necessary sensation to keep us in a problem-solving mode, which enhances our chance of survival, but is at odds with maintaining happiness. So emotional repression is actually a purposeful experience for survival, but it diminishes the possibilities of gaining wisdom and understanding the true nature of our existence. And it certainly stops one essential ingredient in the evolution of advanced human thought, and that is the unleashing of our compassion.

As life progresses, this repression leads to a growing fear of the external world, so the Problem-Solving Mind is obsessed with protecting itself from what it feels is the cause of its discomfort. This is why the information that the external world has presented it with plays such a major role in its attempt to define itself. Our identity is therefore created from what we fear having, or not having, which again leads to emotional repression, as our mind gets stuck in a narrow and focussed pathway of thought. This is why we all carry around an inner sense of dislike for ourselves. That dislike is created from being trapped in a confined perceptual place. This is also why we are obsessed with needing acknowledgment from other people, in order to try and counteract the discomfort. But all the approval in the world will not change the reality of where our lives are housed and what they are being guided by.

The identity that we ultimately hold onto is not the happy successful one, but the insecure one, as we live in a dark, small and lonely world of fear . . .

Our life story!

The very identity we hold onto is the same one that we spend our lives trying to get away from, and this is because of the pain this creates and accumulates.

The Problem-Solving Mind

This may be a good time to ask the following question and reflect upon the answer. How healthy, balanced, flexible and appropriate was your learning?

What was your answer?

Because whatever it was, I assure you that it has created the greatest level of influence on how you perceive yourself in the world in which you exist, whether you know it or not.

Now for the real catch 22 in all of this . . .

Even if your learning was perceived to be healthy and balanced, it doesn't change the fact that your life is still being guided by a very small amount of what is possible to know. You will still be experiencing the very limited version of life that the Problem-Solving Mind is offering you in the Construct – within your life story!

Whether our learning is perceived as healthy or not, the reality is we are still living in a box!

This is why people in general always feel that their life has a restricted sensation, as if something is not quite right. This sensation always leads us to believe that there is something more within us needing to be experienced and expressed. So our Problem-Solving Mind unwittingly sends us on a journey to chase something that does not exist. That way we will never find the real 'version' – the truth of our existence.

There is more to be experienced - lots more! It is not within the confines of our current abode.

It is in the Problem-Solving Mind's interest to function the way it does, because this helps it to maintain its level of control over the world that it has created within its own mind, and to maintain control over us.

If we believe there is no reality just perception, or conversely, if we think our perception is reality, then we will continue to live our lives trapped within a very narrow realm of existence. Therefore, we will never fully experience the true essence of what we are, we will always feel disgruntled with life, eternally dissatisfied, with just brief moments of pleasure. Always thinking that it is our life circumstances causing the discomfort - and most of the time it isn't!

How do we get out of this confined space?

Listen, look, feel, learn and . . . WAKE UP!

Wake up from our deep slumber and journey into the real world! Waking up means becoming aware of all I present. It is real. It does exist. And it is happening. There is a force controlling our lives that overall we are unaware of, even though we know something is not quite right!

My problems are real!

At times when I have presented this topic to people, they have opened their mind to accept that they possibly live in a perceptual reality. However, interestingly they still argue that their problems are real. This is because our most overwhelming and powerful emotions get triggered when we decide that something is a problem, or when we solve a problem.

> **The greater the problem, the greater the emotional pain**
>
> **and**
>
> **the greater the problem, the greater the emotional reward when it is solved . . .**

The Problem-Solving Mind

> hence the encouragement for us
> to find a solution.

Nevertheless, this emotional roller coaster creates the ideal scenario for the Problem-Solving Mind to keep us trapped within its confines and identifying with it as being us.

> As long as we think our problems are real then
> our lives will always feel like a problem.

Now think about this:

> A problem is just a perception.

> So if a perception is not reality, a
> problem is not real.

> Therefore, there are no such
> things as problems.

Problems are just perceptual illusions created by the Problem-Solving Mind. As long as we continue to see life as a problem or any aspect of it as a problem, then we will continue to recruit the power of pain. We will continue to feel the incredible discomfort that is associated with being in a problem-solving mode.

Remember, if we didn't feel uncomfortable about things we wouldn't bother to problem-solve in the first place.

> Stop seeing life as a problem and you
> might just see life. But be prepared, as
> you may not like what you see!

So here we are together on planet Earth, all individually running around thinking that life is a problem that needs solving. Our government leaders have decided that they know, in their almighty wisdom, which issues are the real problems and that we should trust them and let them take control for our own benefit. Now, despite the fact that *Big Brother* is out there protecting us, we poor, meagre little individuals who can't wield such a big stick, are left thinking that the problems our minds have identified, must also be solved in order for us to survive. Now we are stuck, not just in a place of permanent dissatisfaction, but also in a place of being at the mercy of the very system that is supposedly designed to protect us.

What an absolute muddle of insanity that we have got ourselves caught in!

The little individual in this totally de-powered state needs to turn their attention and controlling ways onto something. Inevitably, guess who bears the brunt of their misunderstood frustrations? More than likely, anybody or anything that they are close to in physical proximity, or that they have an intimate relationship with, whether that is at home or at work.

So insanely, off we go on our day-to-day journey through life, trying to work out which problems need solving in order to feel better. In the process of this, we play childlike games of emotional control for the purpose of regaining our falsely identified place of power. Well good luck on this journey, because unfortunately there is no light at the end of this tunnel.

The Problem-Solving Mind leads us down a tunnel that gets narrower and darker until we will no longer be able to see life at all.

To varying degrees, everybody is running around controlling somebody or something and avoiding facing the truth of their own behaviour and the corresponding consequences – and this is clearly evidenced in the fact that the majority of people on this planet refuse to recognise the insanity and cruelty attached to the way we treat, use, abuse and kill animals for our pleasure, progress and survival.

The Problem-Solving Mind

In reality, life cannot be continually dealt with in all of its individual little bits and pieces, as everything is connected. Therefore, every single aspect you change will have varying degrees of effect on something else. Then this secondary aspect of change will affect another factor and so on it goes.

The best way to look at this is not as a sequence of events, but rather as an inevitable reality that already exists, as everything is all one thing anyway, and that one overall experience is the story of our lives. Damaging or changing one aspect of life will definitely affect the overall system in ways that we will never be able to predict or control.

We don't need to predict anything if we allow our minds to move beyond its obsession with outcomes.

Even if you appear to have found a solution to a problem, it will simply push the real issues under the surface where they cannot be seen. Therefore, the forces and energies behind these undealt-with realities seek and build their own misguided direction towards their own form of domination and control.

Without the injection of educated awareness and compassion, the Problem-Solving Mind will continue to dig the human species into a quagmire of mess, that one-day will deny us ever finding an answer to anything, because we will no longer exist.

However, life is throwing signs and clues at us all over the place. Before we precede one more step into the future, I suggest that we wake up to the realisation that we have the power to redirect the Problem-Solving Mind. But, we must first stop and see that it is the Problem-Solving Mind that has created the situation we are now currently trying to deal with.

There is no point continuing with the process of controlling and rearranging what we have created, until we first learn to function and channel the energy of life through an unedited reality.

Stop asking the Problem-Solving Mind to fix the chaos, because it built the chaos that gives its existence purpose.

Chaos is simply a representation of what happens when people see life as a problem, and without chaos, the Problem-Solving Mind would have no purpose. We only see life as a problem when we don't understand it.

Chaos is life not understood.

However, it can be all understood. There is in reality no such thing as chaos – it is an illusion. It is in the Problem-Solving Mind's interest to see life as a problem. We have always been in denial of the truth that life is not a problem, but in reality, it just is what it is.

Reflect on the following:

A question often posed to me from people who are looking at the cruelty and destruction of life is, "if I don't see anything as a problem then I would not do anything about anything, so how do I find motivation in life?" They care deeply about the fact that humanity is on a destructive course, and the cruelty this leads to. However they feel that if this were not seen as a problem then they would not act on these feelings, resulting in a lack of integrity on their part.

That is a great question and yes, there is a clear answer.

If they live outside the Construct and the pain that the Problem-Solving Mind uses to maintain this structure, then they are receiving unedited and clear information about the status of the life they are experiencing. This will still trigger painful emotions because they are caring and compassionate, and the truth is that the world is consumed by pain. There is a lot of denial in regard to the cruelty we inflict upon disadvantaged people and animals. The key is for them to shine awareness on these feelings and to not attach them to their reservoir of pain – their life story. In this

The Problem-Solving Mind

process they will continue to explore what they feel until they sense truth in what they are experiencing. They now understand what they are seeing, rather than just being responsive to it and therefore restricted by their own experiences. This is now emotion embodied with awareness, not delusional pain. They can now compare this to the disturbing way they were approaching 'problems' before. This will lead to empowered motivation to act, but not for the purpose of getting control, or for changing others. Rather to share the awareness of what it is they can see, in whatever format they are skilled to do so, and then what will be will be.

These people can now rest easy in a place of honesty and comfort in knowing that they are doing the best they can. They can't do any more than allow the truth of who they are to connect with the truth of life, and then let the chemistry of this connection create the response. They have now removed themselves from the process of making a choice. Choices are simply not necessary when one is aware. For choices mean giving something up to get something else, and this creates stress, which feeds the notion that life is a problem that needs solving.

Now their life will feel purposeful, but they will not be stressed about what they do, as they let go of perceived outcomes and the need to be right. However, it is important to note that it is not about not feeling pain. If there is pain to be felt then awareness will allow you to absorb this, but only if your reality is big enough and expansive enough. So think bigger than your existing beliefs! What it won't do is drag you deeper into your life story and empower the Problem-Solving Mind's control over you.

They are now Conscious Awareness rather than Conscious Energy trapped inside pain.

Surely we are improving

Many people try and debate with me that the world is improving dramatically and they have great evidence of this; whether it be in the area of human rights, animal protection, environmental initiatives, or technological advances.

Don't jump to any quick conclusions.

To truly test the status of humanity we must look within the realms of every individual's mind and the outward behaviour this is creating.

Fear levels are higher than ever and people are suffering psychologically as they never have before. We are all scrambling to try and make sense of what is going on, thinking that we can keep problem-solving our way out of this mess, or even worse, by making out that we are not trapped in a world of pain in the first place. Sadly and inadvertently, we are just going to dig ourselves into a hole so deep that we will never be able to climb out.

If you are starting to get some sense of how the Problem-Solving Mind functions and how it controls our lives, then continue reading and travel back through your own journey of learning into the mind of a baby.

PHASE FIVE

In the mind of a baby

PHASE FIVE

Our lives start within the safe confines of our mother's womb. Upon exiting this place of warmth, serenity and security, we are subconsciously programmed to spend our entire existence trying to recreate this dynamic from which our lives were created.

A program that is blinding us from seeing the truth - an illusion that masterfully keeps us trapped in a world of pain and confusion - a pathway of survival that leads us to chase something that does not appear to exist.

Happiness!

At least not in the manner that we think it does! In here lies the key to our freedom and to the next phase of our existence.

From the beginning

If we would like our lives to make more sense, then first we must understand what it is that is currently controlling our existence, determining the outcomes of our behaviour, and the manner in which we are experiencing our lives.

So let's go right back to the beginning and see how this all started.

Since the time of our conception the ingredients required for making the Problem-Solving Mind were put in place.

Innocently, within the mind of an unborn child, neural pathways are forming and intertwining. They are developing to generate the necessary functioning in order to create the best possible scenario for survival outside of the womb. Once leaving the confines of this warm and safe haven, the Problem-Solving Mind's job is in motion. It instantaneously knows that this new environment is something that must be readily understood for the continuance of its life. At this early stage it is relatively confused, and the vehicle in which it is housed is physically capable of very little.

A human baby at birth, unlike many other creatures, is totally vulnerable and dependent upon the care of its parents or guardians. It does not intellectually know what this means, but it is certainly programmed to call out for protection and security in the hope that somebody is listening.

The Problem-Solving Mind has no understanding of its external environment at this phase of human development. It must use whatever techniques it can to be looked after while it goes on its journey of analysis. It does this in order to determine the necessary processes of functioning that it needs to survive in this new and comparatively harsh world in which it finds itself.

With all of the information the Problem-Solving Mind receives and analyses via its access to the body's five senses, it builds a belief structure – what I will regularly refer to as the Construct. This structure will form the framework from which the Problem-Solving Mind will guide all of its decision-making throughout the entirety of its existence. In simplistic terms, it is creating a picture of all that it experiences. It does this by attaching various emotions to memories so that it can ascertain in the future, what aspects of life create emotions on the spectrum between good and bad. Obviously it is programmed to move away from bad feelings and move towards good feelings – of course not knowing at this stage that good and bad feelings are all created by pain.

The Problem-Solving Mind learns by association for the purpose of guiding its emotional responses in a more focussed manner.

Here is an example of learning by association: If a baby had an extremely scary experience with a bright red object it is quite possible that anything that is the colour red could potentially trigger a sensation of fear and confusion for the rest of its life. Chances are the child would never learn to understand that this had happened and could therefore inadvertently attach other elements to this fear by association. Without the appropriate guidance from a carer in an aware state, a child's learning may be very convoluted and complicated, leading them to an extremely distorted and irrational fear-based structure of learning to guide their adult life.

So learning by association is a survival technique that leads to the ongoing creation of our perceptions and ultimately our belief structure. A completed belief structure will take some time to create. While a baby is so physically fragile, it must learn very quickly how to use whatever information it has to bring the attention of other humans to its needs. The first time that a baby attempts to control its external environment is when it cries and screams. At this point its lungs and vocal cords are its most equipped piece of survival machinery. As it turns out, this technique is extremely effective and adults are certainly programmed to respond.

A baby has had its first lesson in getting what it wants!

Yes, this is a very innocent process at this point, but how it develops from here is where things start to get very interesting and potentially corrupt.

For obvious reasons, a young baby has no concern for anything other than itself. As we place no expectations on it to do otherwise, this 'selfishness' seems harmless and almost quaint in an innocent young mind. This is our first glimpse at the essence of what drives the Problem-Solving Mind to the state of functioning that we see within adults today. The Problem-Solving Mind at this stage is not built to genuinely care about anything other than itself and this very factor is essential for the survival of an infant. This is also why the Problem-Solving Mind is such a dangerous mechanism of functioning when it is still running the life of an adult human being, particularly when they have access to greater levels of power and control.

This process starts the evolution of the illusion of choice and control.

The infant is very quickly learning what techniques work and what techniques do not. It does this in order to have it needs met as it analyses and absorbs all of the information that life presents. This early phase of learning can have a massive influence on the development of the Problem-Solving Mind and all that it creates. This is why the quality of guidance that an adult is giving to a child is so connected to that person's behavioural characteristics as they grow into a physically mature being.

The more love and basic necessities that a baby receives, the more relaxed the Problem-Solving Mind becomes, and therefore the more capable it is of learning about the true nature of its reality.

It does not take long before that little baby is a young child. It is now physically mobile and capable of expressing its opinions and needs in a fairly complex, detailed and forceful manner. This is the crucial phase for the child to learn that there is far more to life than just its own concept of self, and that its techniques of control must be replaced with intelligent communication and an appreciation for all of life.

To achieve this, a child needs to learn that life is not something to fear, but rather something to embrace, for it is the sensation of fear that continually recruits the ongoing cycle of control that the Problem-Solving Mind is trapped in. If the necessary encouragement for healthy emotional expression is not available to a child, then it will continue to develop techniques that it used as a baby, hence creating more and more disturbing tantrums.

As a child gets older it will use sophisticated emotional techniques of control in order to get what it wants - like emotional guilt, physical intimidation, being nice, sexuality and an array of other masterfully created processes of manipulation. If this process is not curbed then the child will simply take these techniques into their functioning as an adult. By this stage it is a very difficult process to change, let alone recognise, as the Problem-Solving Mind now has a firm grip on the person's existence. The person now thinks it is the Problem-Solving Mind, so it will defend any perceived threats to its existence. It will take everything personally and will find it difficult to receive help.

The transition for a child to learn how to function beyond the parameters of the Problem-Solving Mind is such a crucial phase and can be a very disturbing one for the child and its carer. This is probably why most people avoid it, and sadly turn to increased levels of control or over-nurturing to keep the child in order. Even love in isolation is no longer satisfactory. It must now also be attached to high levels of strength and wisdom. This is necessary in order to guide the child slowly but surely out of a mode of attention seeking and drama, into a world of awareness, compassion and integrity. This transition takes place over many years, until the child is guided towards embarking on its own journey, beyond the need for controls as the mind can now function with integrity. The child in this instance would have been guided to become Consciously Aware.

Think about the ramifications of these divergent possibilities of how a child could grow and learn – awareness enables the ability to feel all that we encounter.

So if we could feel the pain of something, then we would help it, and if we could feel the joy we would share it - this is living in the truth! Destruction, denial and cruelty are simply not possible in such a place of existence.

Are we doing this? Are we living this way? It is adults that are creating the lives that our children will be experiencing . . .

That's a lot of power!

We are abusing this power and corrupting our children, because we don't have the courage to face the truth of our own existence. It is obvious that this essential phase of development has been neglected in the processes of learning that we see today throughout the world.

Even parents that have attempted to bring up their children in a healthy and intelligent manner do not realise that they too are primarily a manifestation of their Problem-Solving Minds. They are therefore inadvertently teaching their children to become a manifestation of the same piece of machinery. They are still using fear as the guide, just in a different disguise. This leaves the child with no other choice but to develop more complex techniques of control, as it knows no other way to function. In the main it is control that parents use to get what they want and this behaviour is what the child absorbs as a template for its own life.

Most children are heading off into life totally confused and bamboozled by the disturbance that is felt as a consequence of living in the Problem-Solving Mind. Or even worse, they actually go through a period where they take advantage of living inside this part of the brain and focus their attention on the competitive pathways of achievement and success. Even though children are often deluded and brainwashed by adults (into thinking that this is the intelligent choice), they are actually just feeding the pain that will one day destroy their spirit.

Bring it on!

The competitive spirit that we so heavily applaud in today's world is simply a by-product of the functioning of the Problem-Solving Mind. As it lives in a permanent state of insecurity it thinks that winning is the answer to life and survival. It therefore has little concern for who must lose in order for it to win. Of course this leads to great levels of achievement and skilful performances that inspire and entertain us - but the people that inspire us are also lost and confused. So who and what are we really following and competing with?

> To take pleasure in success is to take pleasure in other people's failures, for success is only a relative concept.

Meaning, that what we decide is success is primarily dependent on the nature of our learning, and it is therefore just part of our perceptual reality.

> As all perceptions require a point of comparison to exist, success therefore requires a point of comparison of failure.

The Problem-Solving Mind hides this truth behind convenient segregation of its integrity. It is essential that we first learn to enjoy being us outside of the world of comparison and success. Then take this knowing to our children so they can enjoy the process of being alive, the process of giving which enables healthy receiving, as opposed to imposing themselves on life because of the illusion they have fallen victim to. The illusion that happiness (which is a relative concept) can only come from knowing that one's situation is better than another.

This is an illness that has infected many people's current concept of success, achievement and competition.

We live in a world obsessed with receiving - not giving.

This competitive nature was the essence for why we survived and it may be the essence of our demise.

Children develop most of their emotional control techniques from their parents or other key individuals, and this reality turns right back in our faces because we do not wake up to what is going on. The end result is an eternal power struggle between children and parents, or children and any authority figure, and eventually between adults of different belief structures. This leads to nothing but the continuance of the Insanity of Humanity - a situation where one Problem-Solving Mind is pitting itself against another; once again exposing the competitive nature of this part of the brain when guided by pain and fear.

The *game* of life gets perceptually more complicated and serious as we get older; we incorrectly conceive a notion of ourselves being more mature. The transition from childhood emotional control techniques through to a process of waking up our Consciousness is simply not taking place. Most of us have become the victims of a competitive world dominated by pain, fear and control - dominated by the Problem-Solving Mind.

What we are witnessing today is effectively a child's mind trapped in a continually ageing and deteriorating physical body. The mind when trapped in this mode becomes increasingly disturbed and fearful. With time it realises that no matter how much it attempts to control life, or other people, it never seems to be able to find the strength, security, happiness, inner peace and confidence which it so desperately desires.

Blinded by fear

Our infatuation with life extension and finding the eternal fountain of youth is driving us further away from the truth and closer to a place of eternal pain and misery. It is only the Problem-Solving Mind that cannot come to grips with the deterioration of its physical being. Therefore the general theme is that we are becoming more disturbed as we get older, rather than developing the necessary wisdom to age gracefully. As this is an obvious manifestation of today's society, we are also witnessing the increasing speed in which children are becoming psychologically disturbed.

We 'adults' are quickly transferring our increasing levels of fear and pain into the reality of our children's existence. We are inadvertently teaching them to become reliant on their Problem-Solving Minds, as they attempt to find a way out of the madness we have created for them.

When a child is young and vulnerable, they definitely need the Problem-Solving Mind to survive. They also correctly believe that they need other people to look after them in order to feel secure. However, they incorrectly presume that the information adults are feeding them is clear, accurate and pertaining to the reality of their personality structure and environment in which they exist. We then wonder why children today are so disrespectful towards adults, when all they have been presented with is fear and confusion in a deceitful world of denial and mental weakness. Then as these children grow up they are condemned for not behaving with integrity!

The general theme today is that children of all ages are feeling lost and confused and are even becoming subject to quite advanced psychological conditions very early on in their lives. This leaves them with the obvious conclusion that the external world is responsible for how they feel. Therefore an outsider is always to blame when their needs are not being met. And coming from a child's mind, one could say they have every reason to be angry. Today's adults have not supplied them with the most basic and necessary information for them to be able to cope in this world. Remember, this is a child I am talking about, yet this simple process of thinking seems to be very reminiscent of how most adult's function today. We have created a world of blame and transference of responsibility onto the shoulders of somebody other than ourselves and to top it off we have created a system (the law and law enforcement) to feed this notion. Why? Because we have not learnt to handle our own pain and are inadvertently letting this pain guide the functioning of the Problem-Solving Mind.

Children need to be encouraged to feel and explore their existence in order to grow into it, so they can become healthy and aware adults for when they have children and hence create a sustainable and compassionate society for generations to come.

PHASE SIX

The Construct

PHASE SIX

I sit in awe of the Construct, yet within it I feel like nothing, desperately trying to be something, not knowing that nothing is part of everything.

Welcome to the Construct . . .

Welcome to Cyber World.

Have you ever been in a situation in life where you feel like you just want to escape?

One where you are screaming out in your mind, 'Get me out of here!'

If you have, then what you are feeling is your Construct contracting around you. It is an intensified version of that niggling feeling that something is not quite right. It is your Problem-Solving Mind telling you to change the dynamic surrounding you, or that you should remove yourself from it immediately. However, if you sit in that feeling rather than respond to it, this is your chance to see your masterfully designed box of intertwined thoughts – a cage that maintains your incarceration in an illusionary world.

So let's examine the nature of this prison:

Life on planet Earth is not as it seems!

The Construct is quite possibly one of the greatest creations that we will ever have the occasion to witness, and we are inside it right now.

Although we are absorbing information from the external world, we are not actually in it as such. Our lack of awareness leads us on an insatiable journey to rearrange the external world in an attempt to find meaning and happiness. All we are actually doing is rearranging thoughts in our minds. It is this disparity in the awareness of what we think life is compared to what it actually is, that leads to many of the disturbing feelings we experience. We just keep acting on these feelings by trying to change what is perceptually outside of us, as if it is not us creating these uncomfortable feelings in the first place. But even what appears to be outside of us, is in fact inside us!

So what is going on?

Our lives are housed within the realms of a structure that has been created and constantly enhanced by the Problem-Solving Mind. The Construct creates the illusion that our lives are restricted to definable realities, to time, the physical realm and a linear pathway of thought that manifests into our beliefs.

Wherever you are right now, take a moment to stop and look around you.

What do you see?

A house, trees, people – what do you think these things are relative to your personal experience of life?

The truth embodied in the answer to this question could be one of the most important concepts that you or anyone else could ever hope to grasp, if you are to expand beyond fear.

It is not the external world that we are seeing; it is our Construct, a cyber version of life that is *projected* onto the inside of our mind. We are experiencing a complex interpretation of our own thoughts - thoughts that are created in response to information that our mind absorbs via our five senses. This information is edited and arranged to create a picture that we have come to believe is real life, and also the parameters of our existence. These parameters determine the nature of our ability to feel, including what we feel, how we feel it and how we express it.

The Construct is our experiential reality.

This picture, our perceptual reality, continues to evolve with time and creates what we have identified as our life story. Within this life story is everything that we believe life to be, including who and what we are and how we fit into this picture. So our life story, which feels like a journey through time, is in fact just a conglomeration of information, thoughts and feelings, to form the cage that we believe are the parameters of our existence.

This clever Construct of pain-imbued thoughts leads us on an illusionary journey under the false belief that our lives are not actually held captive within a confined space. No matter what we do in this space we are still at the mercy of the dynamics that are necessary to keep this structure in tact. One of those dynamics is that we always feel enough dissatisfaction to believe that our happiness lies ahead of us, in the disguise of a solution to an identified problem. So we feel like we are travelling forward through life, getting closer and closer to a place where life will make sense.

Unfortunately, this is an illusion. We are effectively running around in circles.

We are living our lives within the constraints created by the emotions we have attached to our life story and our beliefs. So our ability to feel is guided by this reality. Yet it is feelings that we crave, hence the need to find success or happiness. But all we find is a regurgitation of our existing emotions in the disguise of a different situation. We are running around inside a process of thought where the things we are looking for do not exist in any tangible sense, but the Problem-Solving Mind creates the illusion that they do, by giving us brief moments of pleasurable feelings. Owing to the pain that we are swimming in within this structure, these lures, although out of reach and obscure, become very tempting to chase. If you would like some advice, then . . .

Stop looking for happiness and start looking at the Construct!

Do you want proof that we are running around in circles?

Examine the last 2000 years in the development of human civilisation. Would you consider that to be a reasonable amount of time for an intelligent species to work out the nature of their existence, to be continually getting wiser and therefore more peaceful in their interaction with life?

I would say that a fair answer would be yes!

The truth is in fact the complete opposite, whether we want to admit it or not. Fear levels are higher than ever before as we face all sorts of terrifying consequences of our own behaviour.

Is there a clear reason as to how this could be possible?

Yes there is. We do not know where we are, so therefore no matter what we do we are getting no closer to learning how to peacefully interact with life, which includes each other and our own sense of being.

So it does not matter what we create within our minds and what we use our minds to create in the external world, we are still stuck in our minds - stuck in the Construct!

The Construct is a purpose-built survival machine and I assure you that it is not guiding your survival with your best interests in mind.

Effectively what we are experiencing is all happening inside our minds!

We are not seeing life itself, but just one specially crafted version of it, based on a point-by-point linear decision-making thought process created by the Problem-Solving Mind. It is a version of life that we believe is life because we have never experienced anything to the contrary. The Construct is distorting our ability to know what it is that we are actually seeing and where we really are. Do not underestimate what I am saying here, for what I am proposing is potentially life-changing if you truly think about the ramifications of bringing this into your awareness.

We identify ourselves through our life story and devote our life to defending and protecting it, even if it is embodied with great pain and confusion. It is pain that was used to guide the creation of the very structure in which we exist. The interesting aspect of limiting ourselves to this confined space is that we feel like we are trapped in a box, a psychological cage that stops our ability to genuinely interact with life – and from that point of view, we are right! So people can feel it, they just don't know what it is they are feeling, so it is important to learn how to feel and how to inject these feelings with awareness. As long as we are unaware of the existence of the Construct, life will continue to feel this constrained.

Of course life continues to change, as do we, but the pain just keeps increasing while the size of the box decreases as we attempt to maintain control.

We all desire to have our lives under control, yet this requires restricting life to feel safe, which means our experiential reality is smaller, meaning our emotions are limited. It is through our emotions that we experience life. Hence life has a very restrictive feeling as we desperately try to problem-solve our way out of our seemingly unsolvable emotional mess. The more we continue to see life as a problem the greater the strength of the Construct, keeping us trapped in its world of illusionary beliefs. When I propose this to people they generally think they are looking at the external world. They open their minds as far as to accept that they may be creating a different interpretation of life, after they first see a truthful version of it. However, that is still not right, but close, as the truthful version is yet to be revealed to us.

We are actually looking at what could be described as a continuous movie playing on the inside of our minds and we have front row seats. This movie cinema is like no other that we have ever experienced before, for this one is fully interactive. It allows us to experience a whole array of sensations and emotions to accompany the visual image. This is the ultimate journey through a virtual reality. We have become so enthralled and overwhelmed by this sensory overload that we are effectively rendered to an incapacitated state.

> **We are effectively asleep and yet somehow still experiencing this cyber world as if it is real.**

The strange niggling sensation that something is not quite right gets locked away. It almost seems insignificant compared to the emotional depth that is dragging us towards an apparent destiny we cannot define. A destiny that inadvertently strengthens the Construct – a belief structure we think we need to stay sane.

> **So in our search for sanity we are actually driving ourselves deeper into our insanity.**

We do not realise it but this life is not ours. We are still in the movie cinema thinking we are making choices and building a life that represents us.

> **That is where the story started for us and could potentially end for humanity.**

The idea that we have entered into a movie cinema may sound like a fictitious story. But this is effectively what has happened to us. It is a cinema that creates such an overwhelming amount of emotional stimulus that we have not gained the necessary awareness to understand what and where we are.

Conscious Energy exists in a realm that is so overwhelming in its connection to the physical and emotional aspects of life that we never fully recover. Hence we have never been able to work out why we entered this realm in the first place.

> **We are the essence of awareness living inside a sensory world of thoughts, emotions and images.**

Conscious Energy has found a portal to life through the human mind, but it can't figure out how to get out of the mind while still maintaining consciousness, and hence our life as we know it.

Now imagine the human spirit, as Conscious Energy, waking up in the midst of the mind of a human baby. Imagine experiencing the physical realm through the five senses for the first time ever. It would be so overwhelming that you would actually forget who and what you are. You would effectively become the feelings and sensations that you are experiencing and you would never learn to move beyond that.

We have become trapped within the confines of the Construct; a cyber sensory reality, which just like in the movie is not real, yet we believe it is. Keep in mind when I say 'real' I am referring to life in an unedited state. Anything smaller than this (meaning an edited version) only exists within the framework of perception.

This does not sound too bad does it - living in a realm of deep emotions and sensory stimulation? If only it was that simple.

I'm not suggesting that we shouldn't live within our Construct of functioning; I am simply pointing out that this is where we reside. However, be mindful, should we choose to stay in this realm there are certain parameters we will have to learn to live with. The greatest of which is pain and the fear that it creates as the Construct is guided by nothing else. If we live in the Construct our life will be limited to what our fear allows us to experience, a small and distorted version of what is possible.

Pinhole Theory

All the information that we are utilising and therefore experiencing is a pinhole relative to what's possible. This is information pertaining to our 'story' of what was, what is and what could be. It is constructed from our fear-based learning (an edited version of life) so our life story is much smaller than we think. Yet it is our life story that feels so huge, to the point that it disables us from truly understanding and feeling life beyond this. It doesn't matter whether our perception of the information in the story is negative or positive. Of course it will be a combination of both, which in reality adds up to the same thing within all of us. Meaning, in the Construct, the Problem-Solving Mind attempts to maintain a balance between positive and negative thoughts for the purpose of maintaining control and keeping the illusion of our life story alive.

If we put too much effort into creating positive thinking, the mind will eventually force the balance back by creating an overwhelming and uncontrollable amount of negative associations and thoughts. The reason for this is because such a small amount of information, relative to what has been originally absorbed, requires a lot of management and control to keep it in such a restricted place of existence. The Construct is in a constant process of rearrangement while the Problem-Solving Mind desperately tries to maintain its structural integrity. It does this under the falsely identified bombardment of life's new information. So it is easy to see why we always feel stressed as we cram the entirety of life into our Pinhole of a story!

Whatever one is thinking and whatever the nature of those thoughts, it is important that we stay aware that it is still just a version and all versions are created by pain. Pain, when housed in the Construct, turns into nothing but fear, disguised behind various thoughts and beliefs. All we are guiding our lives by is a restricted version of what is first absorbed. We will never see or experience what life actually is if we stay housed within the Construct.

All we experience is the 'outcome' of the Problem-Solving Mind's analysis of the external world.

We live our lives obsessed with outcomes, because without realising it, we are trapped in a world of nothing but outcomes.

As our Pinhole gets smaller the pain of absorbing and filtering life will intensify. This is because we are trying to maintain a version that is becoming increasingly smaller than what it actually is. We will then attempt to withdraw from life in order to cope.

The Construct

This reduces the amount of information that is challenging our concept of existence; hence the desire to stay within 'known' boundaries in our lives.

This still serves the objectives of the Problem-Solving Mind's pain driven processes, as it ultimately still has us fooled into believing that what we are experiencing is the entirety of what is possible. In fact we end up feeling like we are absorbing too much – but in reality we are absorbing very little and inadvertently this is where the distorted pain comes from. The Construct continues to intensify the belief that the external world is causing our pain, so it keeps us far away from anything that would allow us to evolve into Conscious Awareness – or at least it appears that way.

As we decrease the size of our Pinhole the pain will increase, because we don't realise that to free ourselves requires the complete opposite approach - to absorb, feel and embrace all of life's information. Even though this is an ever-changing reality, we can in this instance embrace the change and the constant absorption of wisdom. In fact it will make life feel so alive that we will just open our minds wider and wider until there is no Pinhole at all – we are now absorbing everything that is. And then life will just make sense as it could not be any other way and the illusion that we have choices disappears. We would then embrace the ever-changing newness of life and let go of the control that our Problem-Solving Mind has told us we need to survive.

The purpose of choice is to navigate the Construct, not life!

The reason most people reject the proposition that we could live beyond our Pinhole existence, which effectively is our Construct, is because of the enormity of our pain. And as mentioned, this convinces us that we are actually receiving too much information; an overload of information compels us to dig a deeper hole to protect ourselves.

In accepting that we are actually living in a small and distorted perceptual place of existence, the true Insanity of Humanity is exposed as we devote all of our energy into playing psychological games with each other rather than understanding how to absorb the truth of life. Let's now look deeper into the nature of the concept of a game, because in essence that is what we are living within.

The Game

Games can only be played when certain rules and parameters are followed. That is exactly how the Construct functions and why it can be observed and understood. So it's very important for us to become familiar with the nature of The Game in which we are trapped, rather than unwittingly playing The Game. If we continue to do that, then we have been fooled – tricked into thinking this is what life is all about, when in fact this could not be further from the truth.

Within the structures of the systems we have created, we have developed many games to play so people can pit their skills against one another. It would appear that it is very important for us to feel that we are good at something, as this is an obvious mode to enhance our chances of survival. We have made this a relative concept and to feel this way we must be better than someone else; hence the selfish nature of our functioning that blinds us to our own destructive behaviour.

We need there to be a loser for us to feel like a winner in whatever realm we are playing in. So to give us this satisfaction, we search out various means to create the feeling of success within our mind. But the questions to consider are; do we need to fulfil this desire to survive in today's world and where is it currently getting us?

The Construct

This competitive game-driven mentality is no longer necessary as the driving force behind the essence of our behaviour.

It is within The Game of the Construct that the concept of success and achievement is created. It is here that we allow integrity to be sacrificed for such desires to be fulfilled.

People often get fooled into thinking that there are the games that we play (such as sport or various other physical and mental challenges that have various rules and regulations attached to them) and then there is life that we must abide by within the structures of our society. For many people, the latter is not seen as a game, because it has higher stakes attached to it; meaning, these processes of human interaction that occur within the framework of the workplace, government structures and any other attached systems, are necessary for the continuance of our survival.

There are many people who would consider that personal relationships do not fall under the category of a game. However, we are successfully programmed after many years of evolution, to know that our survival relies on creating effective relationships that serve our purpose and inadvertently they become a game of emotional manipulation and deceit.

Life has become all about winning.

But we can't all be winners.

So what aspects of life do we approach as if they are a game?

Give this question the due consideration that it deserves, as I assure you there is more truth lying behind this question than you could have ever possibly imagined.

How would you feel if I proposed that the whole thing is a game?

I mean everything.

Every aspect of our existence in which we partake is in fact just a game; a game that is so shrewdly designed that we can't even get past first base. The reason for this is because we think first base is the entirety of the dynamics that we must deal with.

So let's clarify what I mean by first base. First base represents everything that we currently think life is; it is the cinema of life that we are trapped in. Therefore we never try to go past this, but instead attempt to control and fulfil our desires in the place in which we currently stand.

But this is an illusion.

So what are the necessary requirements to keep this illusion in place?

An important one is that we think some aspects of life are a game and that others are not.

Imagine that I draw a line in the sand; on one side you must place every aspect of your existence that you think is a game, and on the other side you place every aspect of your existence that you think must be taken seriously. Everybody has a different interpretation of which bits and pieces go to which side, and everybody thinks that their version is right and that others are wrong, unless of course somebody else agrees with them.

Look at some of the divergent realms of emotional energy that different people put into different aspects of life. Some people take a game of football so seriously that they can feel absolutely devastated when their team loses. In fact, they can put more emotional energy into this game than they would put into their families, their work or their loved ones. Now to another person this would be seen as insane, as they may propose that this is just ridiculous behaviour and how could anybody get so worked up over a game. To them, for example, they may argue that their job and looking after their family is the only thing that matters, and this is where they must put all of their time, effort and energy.

The Construct

So who is right, both of them, one of them, or none of them?

No one is reading the information of life correctly.

The truth is we are all trapped in a game but The Game is not what we think. Whatever perceptual angles we come from, in terms of what we think is a game or not, whether it is football, personal relationships, the government, the business world, or, dare I say, religion and spiritualty - all of them are just masterfully designed distractions. They keep us directing our attention away from the real issue, hence the truth as to what is actually going on with our lives gets lost.

In the current mode of functioning that we are trapped in, we are just pawns being conveniently used like puppets on a string. Pain via the pathways of the Problem-Solving Mind does everything it can to disallow us from seeing this. The Construct convinces us that if our emotional needs aren't satisfied then our life will be meaningless. So we never sit still long enough to look beyond these emotions as they so powerfully call for action.

Think of being in the Construct, this movie we are watching, as an interactive game. The Construct therefore represents the restrictive barriers of our existence, as it determines every aspect of our experiential reality. It is a representative of what we have defined as evolution. So it serves evolution, not us! It has such control over this process that we think that life can be no other way.

And that is the challenge of this game.

The challenge for all of us is to first realise that we are in The Game. Then we need to learn how to master it.

To master the Construct is probably the greatest challenge we will ever have to face in our entire life. It is a game that is full of information that must be decoded and understood if eternal freedom is our desire. Otherwise we will stay trapped in a permanent state of confinement until the vehicle that we are travelling in ceases to exist.

> **The Construct is the psychological cage that incarcerates our existence. Every one of our beliefs represents another shackle in this mind-made penitentiary.**

Take heed because the Construct is no ordinary prison. It is definitely top security. It is within these confines that we exist. We are playing a game with the wrong rules and we wonder why, no matter what we do, we never seem to win.

Don't get caught up in trying to logically rationalise whether what I'm saying is true or not. What I encourage is that we start getting a sense of a deeper connection to that niggling feeling that something is not quite right. For it is within that feeling that the key to our freedom lies. It all started so innocently and simply as we were drawn into wanting to experience something beyond our existing realm of knowing. Now it has all turned quite awry on us, as we have been drawn into this game of virtual reality where it permanently feels like our very life is at stake.

> **A life that started with wanting is now trapped in wanting, as wanting is just a mode of thinking - an illusionary sense of purpose and growth.**

Emotions and the subconscious world

The reason it is so difficult to see the Construct is because it primarily functions within our subconscious realm. After rapid ongoing strategic analysis of all information the Construct receives, we are then presented with a purpose-built version of it in our conscious realm. This is the edited version of life, hence why it is so difficult for us to fully understand what we are experiencing. If one were to see the entirety of their subconscious world, it would look very different to the world they currently know to be real.

Think about what we currently consider to be the conscious world as the movie cinema we are in. The subconscious world creates the movie and presents it to us in such a manner that we actually think we are making decisions and controlling our lives from our conscious state. But we are not! The gap between the information being received and the creation of the movie is so minute that it feels like we are the creator of our life story. It is not until we have embodied both our subconscious and conscious state into a unified place of awareness, that we can become the creator of our life experience.

This dimension we are in presents a certain amount of information that creates a certain range of emotions or emotional responses - but it is limited. It is not the entirety of what we can actually feel. We are trapped in a restrictive emotional realm that we are not creating. We are only experiencing emotions that are purpose-built to keep us trapped in our psychological cage (the Construct). Our identity is being created through this limited emotional range. Even though we are very capable of feeling more within ourselves, the Construct only allows us to present an expression of self that matches this distorted and restricted sense of being. This leads to ongoing frustration, as people never feel understood and struggle to understand others in a confusing and controlled emotional world.

People in the Construct use emotionally manipulative techniques, because they have such a limited array of emotions to actually cope and survive. To create an effect to present to the world, they have to be clever about which ones they utilise and which ones they don't. As they are incapable of feeling and understanding the entirety of what it is that they are experiencing, it is easy to see why the mind wants to incessantly manipulate life when it is stuck in such a limited restrictive realm - let alone trying to create an identity in it. Think about how we are all creating this identity within that emotional energy and how distorted and confusing this is for all of us, hence the difficulty in connecting with each other in any deep and honest manner.

As our identity is so fragile, we obviously defend it whenever we feel under threat. Not surprising when we think about the restricted and uncomfortable environment in which we have found our existence residing. Even when someone is trying to help us, it feels like they are attacking us because they are proposing emotions and concepts that have no place within our Construct - the home we have identified with and protected for so long.

Given that we are all guided by fear, it is reasonable to propose that we are all living in a small, distorted reality. Therefore, we are all giving off a distorted self, and the information we are going to get back from life is going to be distorted as well. The really crazy part is that we are defining ourselves by the information we get back from life even though we are presenting and receiving distortion right from the beginning - and on goes the cycle of our misguided lives. So there is no start or end as to where the deformation of life comes from. The whole thing is a misrepresentation of truth and we as a species are trying to connect and interact within this.

PHASE SEVEN

Behind Cyber World

PHASE SEVEN

Pulling the mask off to expose The Ego

Lets have a look at one of the most misunderstood terms used so readily in discussions about life and human behaviour - The Ego.

The Ego is the Problem-Solving Mind's attempt to be a human being, to have a personality, to live and experience life, and most importantly to be able to communicate with us through a vision of a physical being that it and we can relate to.

And The Ego's home is the Construct.

In fact whilst living in the Construct we are effectively all functioning under the guidelines of an ego. Think of it as a complex computer program that is actually trying to work out how to be a person. The Ego has the potentially dangerous combination of being scared and confused, while at the same time having access to all of the creative genius that lies within the potential of the Problem-Solving Mind.

The Ego desperately wants to live and experience life and it currently sees us as a threat, while at the same time a very useful source of energy – not to mention an intriguing housemate! Unfortunately, because of this fear of us, most of the time The Ego treats us more like a slave, keeping us trapped in the deeper reaches of its dark passages. It realises we have the power to grab the controls of the vehicle in which we are both housed, as we attempt to find freedom from our bondage. So we and The Ego have a common goal – just very different ways of going about it.

The Problem-Solving Mind has either personally witnessed or gathered information on how we have attempted to separate our spirits from The Ego in the past. For example, many spiritual teachings talk about The Ego as if it is some terrible thing that we must destroy. What do you think The Ego is doing while you read this type of information - just casually sitting back and saying okay, go ahead and take over my world? Of course it isn't, it is taking all of this knowledge in and using it to stop you from killing it. It is creating more advanced illusions and lures to take us all further away from the truth. You can't blame it really, if we have not told it otherwise.

The Ego is desperate to never be seen by us as it would see this as effectively blowing its cover. The Ego therefore creates a whole array of disguises to protect itself from ever being discovered. It is the master of justifications. It uses arguing as a useful tool to confuse other people's minds and avoid being exposed.

The Ego is so clever at never allowing us to see its true face behind its mask that it has created many Cyber Selves to throw us off track. We think The Ego is just an insecure and selfish version of us. In saying this we are very close to seeing the truth.

The error of judgment that many people have made here (which is part of the clever design of the Construct) is that when we are not our ego we are our real selves. The purpose of an ego is to keep us thinking that if we stay away from it, we are being true to this falsely identified real self, otherwise known as our authentic self.

The authentic self is often referred to as an accumulation of our personality and our life experiences – but remember this is just our Pinhole of information that we erroneously think is us. So it is still just another cyber version of us – another layer of the illusion!

Firstly, all of The Ego's aspects previously discussed are simply part of the programmed nature of our existence and are not reality as such, even though they exist. Secondly, these aspects are constantly changing and rearranging for the purpose of survival, as they are all connected to the functioning of the Construct. So if our authentic self is being sold to us in this disguise, then it will simply be another lure that will lead us into further disillusionment, and our life will continue to serve its time in incarceration.

Getting away from our ego does not mean that we are suddenly in touch with the real us and that we are free from Cyber World. There is no such thing as just getting away from our ego. If it was that simple we would have all figured this out a long time ago -

and theories of such a nature have been floating around for many centuries.

If we truly desire to understand our existence, it is so important that we open ourselves to the complex system of illusion that we are either trapped in or struggling to enter. It has many layers and levels to navigate and see through, hence why I emphasise the need to understand the energy that created all of this in the first place. The really challenging part is that we are using our mind to expose the truth that the mind tries so hard to hide – but it can be done!

For the purpose of building the appropriate pathways towards freedom, think of The Ego as a lure that gives us a false sense of understanding of the difference between the world of the mind and the world of the spirit. In the process of giving so much attention to The Ego and all that it creates, we have once again been fooled into a never-ending loop of dissatisfaction. The world outside of The Ego is still within the confines of the Construct. The Ego is just one small part of the equation that we need to understand and learn how to communicate with.

The Ego is the Problem-Solving Mind's human cyber face.

Once we see The Ego for what it really is and stop getting halted at the point of associating with its human qualities, we will start to sense and see the truth of its existence and functioning. Rather than seeing The Ego as something we need to remove the real us from, see it as a gateway into discovering the truth behind the functioning of the Problem-Solving Mind. For at the moment, what we think is the real us, is simply just another cyber version of life, another cyber human being, which is no closer to being real (in the sense that we are trying to discover) than The Ego.

The Ego is simply living proof that the Problem-Solving Mind is in fact an extremely intelligent but very scared child trying to survive and work out this Universe in which it exists on its own.

It needs us to help it create a greater sense of knowing and understanding of its own existence. So obviously to create this scenario of communication, we must first stop fearing it, and secondly stop identifying with all of the information presented to us by the Problem-Solving Mind.

As long as we are in the Construct, all the information we receive from life is just a conveniently edited and manipulated version. This is for the purpose of maintaining the Construct, and for the purpose of maintaining a system of functioning which disallows us from ever seeing the truth of anything. Think about that for a moment . . .

If we are in a perceptual world then we are never seeing the truth.

So life can never make sense - simply not possible.

Yet we enforce our opinions and beliefs despite the distortion of our thinking. We are currently putting in very little united effort as a species to address these realities – other than exploring the theories that offer a quick fix solution with happiness for sale.

We are lost in a concept of ourselves in this world; we will never grow past this notion until we see through the enormous depth and breadth of this illusion, and clearly sense ourselves within it.

I know the existing concept of The Ego and enlightenment are long-held theories, which many people in the world of spiritual teaching have devoted their lives to, so I am not wanting to disrespect any of this. I am just suggesting that there is more to the whole dimension in which we exist than has currently been seen, understood and taught. So if it is necessary for you to continue this journey with me, maybe just explore this section as an interesting proposition before you jump to any conclusions.

Cyber Selves

The guardians of the Construct and The Ego!

At the risk of making this story of the journey of humanity even more complicated, let's take a closer look at the cyber faces that the Problem-Solving Mind creates to protect its human face. Remember, this is all just a cyber reality that we are living in, so the Problem-Solving Mind can create what ever it wants. The only limitation to its creativity comes from its own self-employed limits. These it creates from its lack of understanding of so much that it experiences.

The Problem-Solving Mind currently seems limited to the thought of being a human being and therefore keeps creating as many cyber versions of what it thinks it is in order to deal with life. Remember, whatever it creates and thinks it is, we currently think we are! This is why life feels like an emotional washing machine, where everybody is struggling to work out who they really are as they bounce around from one notion of self to another. If we consider that none of these versions of us are the actual truth, we can then expect a life that is bursting with confusion, unless of course we become Consciously Aware!

The Construct is quite a full house, as there are many different personalities running around attempting to maintain control of this thing called life. As The Ego is the key representative of the Problem-Solving Mind, it likes to stay in the background as much as possible as it sees this as an essential protective measure for its survival.

The world of psychology would like to think that it is only people with advanced and *unhealthy* psychological conditions that are subject to such extreme manifestations, but I assure you every living human being effectively has multiple personalities to deal with different situations in life. The Problem-Solving Mind has been able to create these various Cyber Selves so cleverly we actually slip from one into to the other without even noticing. It does this to ensure it does not spark off our awareness of anything being wrong.

If you want to explore this topic in simplistic terms, then think of all the different social masks that you create to deal with various scenarios in your life.

It does not matter how hard you try, I am sure you cannot maintain a single 'you' to deal with every single circumstance in life. This is why the concept of 'you' is a very complex and confusing one for most people.

So each individual Cyber Self is literally just a program that has been developed from our informative and key learning years during the creation of our Construct. The programs we utilise depend on our fear-based learning, which our Problem-Solving Mind determines will necessitate the highest probability of creating control over its existence, and therefore its survival.

Each Cyber Self uses different emotional control techniques that it learnt when we were children. As these Cyber Selves have been within us throughout the journey of our lives into adulthood, they slowly but surely manifest deeper and more sophisticated personalities attached to these emotionally driven techniques. Of course when they get too complex and powerful, people feel like they are literally going mad.

During the process of absorbing the information I am presenting, observe your own behaviour and the behaviour of others. Take a look at all of the systems we have created and how they are representative of our beliefs, our fears and our many different Cyber Selves. Observe how they are used to disguise the real truth of what we actually feel. Notice how something in us is always trying to protect a deeper state of insecurity and think about whom and what that thing is. This is the face of The Ego, which is the mask for the Problem-Solving Mind, which is driven by pain.

Think about how people have always sensed that politicians are being dishonest to them, that our real-estate agent is not telling us the truth, or that our partner is manipulating us to get what they want. Take a close look at these faces that the world is presenting, for these faces carry the characteristics and essence of the functioning of the cyber reality in which we exist.

It can be seen

To me, what I'm about to share with you is just brilliant in its design and extremely exciting to become aware of.

The Problem-Solving Mind wants us to stay in a world where we think that everybody's mind is different, hence sending us on an insatiable journey of control that fully occupies our time and attention.

> Think about how we all fight for our individuality and yet at the same time fight to be treated the same!

The interesting observation to be made beyond the fact that every single Construct appears outwardly to be totally unique, is that they all, behind the individual personalities and beliefs, show exactly the same characteristics. Even though the disguises they present to the world are all totally different, once you understand the mechanisms of functioning behind them, it is effectively like seeing one entity communicating with you, as opposed to a group of different individuals.

To make myself clear, I am proposing that there is one united force or intelligence that is driving all Constructs and all of our unique and individual minds. This is the Super Construct. Otherwise it would not be observable and predictable in terms of its characteristics of functioning. The best way I could describe it would be to say that the Super Construct is a representative of a living entity and it is using us to express its influence and control over the world. The Super Construct could be described as what some people call Creation and others call Evolution.

The Super Construct is one united thing and our vehicle is being utilised to serve its purpose. This feature is necessary for pain to be able to fulfil its objectives. Otherwise it would not be able to control the destiny of humanity in the manner that we are currently witnessing.

Stop and think about what it would take to head seven billion people down a predictable pathway with an inevitable end result.

And not just that; a pathway we can see being created but feel helpless to stop.

Even though we can observe all of the different faces that the Problem-Solving Mind creates, once we are attuned to what it is we are actually looking for, we realise that all of these different Cyber Selves are actually a representation of one thing. When we understand the nature and functioning of the Construct and the Super Construct, it gives us an opportunity to see where we have been imprisoned, and to understand why it is so difficult to connect with life.

Once we can see this cage of beliefs and programs we have the opportunity to stop identifying with them. Even if it's for one brief moment, this is our chance to see the intelligent life force behind the creation of it all, hence the importance of not totally separating ourselves from it.

I assure you it is there to be seen.

If you can truly sense what I am talking about, you can see that this force functions way beyond the parameters of your Construct. In fact, it exists beyond the confines of space and time and the physical realm to which we have become so heavily reliant upon.

Never underestimate the level of genius that is behind the design of this extraordinary structure. Once it is witnessed for the majesty of its creation, it offers us a glimpse as to the potential of the power of our minds.

Any physical structure that humans have created in the external environment, pale in comparison to a complex system of functioning that is powerful enough to incarcerate and utilise, what I consider to be the most astonishing thing that exists in the Universe, Conscious Energy.

However, the longer the Problem-Solving Mind is able to maintain the Construct, the greater its power becomes and with this you will see external structures that match the functioning of its own internal structure.

Humanity can only hope that we are never foolish enough to allow ourselves to travel to this point, as the consequences for us would be devastating.

As we are a source of energy, we are used to fuel and keep these mechanisms functioning, while the energy attached to the processes of pain and fear are used to keep us believing that the Construct is real. We are effectively trapped in a survival mode that disallows us from looking beyond this realm. In fact in the main we don't even know that we are in it in the first place.

This incredible Construct that we are housed within is only capable of the illusion to beat all illusions, because the human mind, as a piece of machinery, has such an incredible potential for creativity. It has the ability to develop an artificial version of life and can add on an advanced imaginative component beyond any other living creature on earth. As long as it stays in this artificial version, then our existence will just continue to represent a diluted version of how we could potentially exist.

Once we become empowered with the complete awareness of what we are, the Construct no longer exists in the manner in which we are currently experiencing it. This intelligence will be there for us to utilise and guide. But first I suggest that we learn to move beyond the illusion that the Problem-Solving Mind has created.

What I am proposing that we need to do is no simple task, for I am suggesting that we totally stop identifying with every single existing thought and belief that currently drives our lives, and therefore every emotion that we feel – if only momentarily to see what it is I present.

If you have become fully identified with your Construct as being you, then to do this is comparable to asking you to give up your life.

Once again don't be fooled, as this is just another part of the illusion created by the Problem-Solving Mind.

So as stated earlier, owing to the fact that most people have never been guided past the childlike functioning of the Problem-Solving Mind, they erroneously come to the conclusion that this is the only place of functioning for a human being. They therefore continue to develop and enforce their belief structures on all aspects that envelop their lives. As a belief structure is not reality or the truth of life, we are simply walking with arms wide open into the Insanity of Humanity, as we attempt to enforce a distorted fear based version of life onto life itself.

If you can sense the truth in what I am saying to you right now, then this may give you a glimpse of understanding into the nature of the functioning of humanity in the world today.

Human beings on this planet are attempting to enforce 'their way' as if that is 'the way' because they know no other way!

PHASE SEVEN

Putting the pieces together

When you live in the Construct every single thing that you experience is not life itself; you are experiencing the inside of your brain. I know it is a very strange thought to think that you are actually looking around at the parameters and potential of your own mind, but it can also be very empowering.

Look at your body - that's just an image in your mind connected to everything else you see. Therefore, from an experiential point of view we are in fact not separated from anything.

Now I would like you to really investigate the next idea in your mind and see what it brings.

For you to be able to recreate a vision of life inside your mind then everything you can see or experience was already in your mind in the first place - otherwise you would not be able to recognise what you were seeing. It would just be a lot of information that would have no sense or meaning to you whatsoever.

> **We are what we see. We are the Universe in a state of consciousness.**
>
> **Is it possible that we created ourselves to see ourselves for the purpose of understanding ourselves?**

So yes I am implying here that we may have even created the whole thing, including the pain. However, although our minds are withholding the truth to the Universe, this wealth of information remains hidden from our view, because we are so distracted by our misunderstood and powerful emotions.

We are lost in our feelings that only allow us to see life from one perceptual angle at any one point in time. This creates 'The Game' as we lunge from one emotion to another. We do this by rearranging the thoughts in our minds as we try to escape our pain. And we do this not knowing that we are in a maze that has no exit.

It is not a matter of escaping this maze of intertwined fear-based thoughts; it is a matter of realising that it is all an illusion.

We are trapped in an artificial realm of existence. We are trapped in Cyber World. This world is very real but it is not life as such. We are currently limiting ourselves by getting confused as to why our illusionary finite reality in the Construct does not match the infinite realm of life. It never will match. This only serves to work against us when we get stuck trying to keep life's information in a conceptually finite place - within the confines of a belief. Alternatively, imagine if the experiences that we are absorbing were in fact individual pieces, when put together could unlock and decode the Construct. This would then release our minds to the infinite possibilities of life.

So the Problem-Solving Mind is doing its job and it is doing it brilliantly.

However, I would like you to consider the following very carefully . . .

If the Problem-Solving Mind did not challenge us to the degree that it does, then would we ever figure out what is necessary to move beyond our existing imprisonment - why would we bother? Collectively, the pain is increasing and becoming so intense that the confusion it creates is forcing humanity to look beyond all existing notions of what life is and how the brain functions.

The potential for the journey of awakening has only just begun, so enjoy the ride!

PHASE EIGHT

The need to believe

I believe!

Explaining the concept of beliefs is probably where I encounter the most resistance from people. I am sure most people would understand the idea of a belief, or to believe in something. In fact it would be fair to propose that people on the whole would consider that to strengthen our beliefs is one of the most important things we need to do in our lives. Sadly, this is all part of the illusion that we have been drawn into. So it is important to understand how they are created and what their true purpose is.

To live within the realm of beliefs is all that we have ever known, and it is this realm that is driving us deeper into the Insanity of Humanity. This is because it is our beliefs that determine the structural strength of our Construct.

Consider the following:

> **It is not necessary for us to believe in something for it to exist.**
>
> **Therefore it is not necessary for us to believe in anything for us to exist.**

We exist whether we believe in ourselves or not. Life exists whether we believe in it or not. Therefore the continuance of life and us is not dependent on beliefs.

Yet it is beliefs that we have become dependent on.

Beliefs are interesting creations and have been important for our survival as a species, but it is possible to learn to function beyond the limiting parameters they create in our minds.

> **Look at beliefs as a stepping-stone to something else – a platform to leap into the unknown. Not something to hold onto, defend and protect.**

What is a belief?

A belief is our perception of something based on our experiences to do with a particular topic, person, or in fact any aspect of life that we encounter. They are all just individual little stories that require much justification to hold them together – amalgamate them and you have the structure of your life story and your Construct.

A belief is a thought, a concept, a notion, or an idea that the Problem-Solving Mind has attached fear to. Remember that the Problem-Solving Mind sees life as a problem that requires a solution, and coherent with this observation is the fact that it also fears all of life. So it creates beliefs to attempt to deal with what it cannot understand and will never understand within the parameters of its existing functioning.

Although people use their beliefs to guide the entirety of their existence, beliefs only encompass a small aspect of what an individual can experience.

So here we are living our lives limited to our beliefs, and our beliefs are only a limited version of what is, yet somehow we expect that all of life should make sense.

It never will when we are functioning in such a fashion.

Once a thought has manifested into a belief, it becomes part of our mind's structure, which we have falsely identified as being ourselves. We therefore use our beliefs to guide our lives, in an attempt to build an external structure that matches the internal structure of our minds. The Problem-Solving Mind dictates that this process is necessary for happiness to exist. This is where the need to control stems from. The illusion of control that we chase becomes an insatiable journey of ongoing disappointment, confusion and pain.

This confusion is exacerbated by the fact that when we are living within the confines of our Construct, there is in reality no internal or external world. And that is part of the illusion.

See how this thought sits in your mind:

> **In our current mode of existence, there is our internal world that we are stuck in, and we are never actually interacting with anything other than our own thoughts.**
>
> **Let the madness begin!**

Even when another person is talking to us, our mind is hearing and creating an interpretation of their voice after filtering it through our beliefs. Therefore, by the time we actually hear it we are just hearing our own thoughts that we then interact with. This is why effective communication is so difficult. Also this illustrates why it is so important to create a mind with enough awareness that you can experience and interact with an unedited reality.

Within our mind we have a large number of beliefs ranging from some that are very flexible and relatively unimportant (as far as our life is concerned) through to ones that are incredibly solid and rigid. Our beliefs encompass all aspects of what we think and feel life is and they are all pertaining to our notion of survival. We have for example beliefs as to what we look like, our self-worth, other people, life itself, love or God; in fact anything and everything that we experience is somehow attached to, or affected by a belief. The more rigid the belief the more likely it is that we will fight to protect and defend it; therefore the greater the pain we will feel when it is challenged. We don't realise that most of our beliefs exist until they are triggered by either similar or conflicting information from life.

Reflect on your own life right now. Think about what it feels like when somebody challenges one of your stronger beliefs on a particular topic. How does that make you feel? How does that make you feel about them? Do you instantly like them less? Does that make them wrong and you right? Does that justify judging or condemning that person?

As with the functioning of a child, as long as the Problem-Solving Mind is guiding us, we will continue to hold other people responsible for the uncomfortable feelings that are created when one of our beliefs is challenged.

Now think about a time when you have been out socially and you meet someone that has similar beliefs to your own. How does that make you feel? Like life makes more sense? In this situation we are still holding the other person responsible, but this time for feeling good, so in time this still leads to us wanting to control them in order to maintain this feeling.

This is a life lived at the mercy of one's beliefs, a life where you will be continually stressed as the world keeps changing faster than your mind can rearrange its thoughts.

In today's modern world the information that we are receiving from our five senses is changing so rapidly that it is making it very difficult for us to maintain our beliefs and all they represent. This is why most people are suffering such advanced and disturbing psychological conditions. In the not too distant past, life was relatively simple and change was relatively slow from the perspective of one person's lifetime, so maintaining a belief was easier. As this is not the case for us today, it leaves us with some very straightforward options. Firstly, we could attempt to bury ourselves away from life to avoid the pain of trying to adjust to this incredible rate of change. Or secondly, we could fight even harder to enforce our way of thinking to ensure that the rest of the world adjusts to us (good luck on that one). Or thirdly, we could wake up to the reality that it is totally unnecessary to do either, because our beliefs were never you or I right from the beginning. Therefore we don't have to take anything that we see or experience personally. This would allow us to relax and absorb the truth of who we are and the truth of life. Taking life personally obviously limits our ability to absorb the entirety of life as our attention is too heavily focussed on protecting some notion of self – and ultimately the conglomeration of all our beliefs equates to our notion of self, not just the beliefs in regard to our human form and our behaviour.

The reason we don't explore the truth beyond beliefs is because we think we can't live without them, and given that our life story (and our concept of self) lives within beliefs, this is not surprising. In fact we see it as very important to believe in something, particularly ourselves. We see beliefs as holding the solidness and strength that we want to feel. Little do we know that believing disables any chance of this being possible. Having said that, a strong belief can be very purposeful towards the advancement of achievement in a particular field of endeavour, but it has nothing to do with understanding our existence, in fact it's the complete opposite.

So why would we not go deeper into understanding beliefs if we thought they held the key to our salvation? Because we are so caught up in finding something to believe in. We think the fear we feel comes from not believing, not realising that it is actually the process of maintaining a belief that fuels the fear.

Every belief we see in another person could have potentially been a belief that we ourselves ended up with given a certain set of learning experiences. To continue living within the framework of our narrow set of beliefs creates the stress that keeps the role of the Problem-Solving Mind alive, as we continue to resist and control beliefs that appear to be different to our own.

> **Effectively a belief is just a carefully constructed thought in our brain; it is part of the illusion, yet we are living as if we are our beliefs.**

And because we think we are our beliefs, we will stay immersed in a world of power struggles and confusion. Not to mention that all of our beliefs put together only represent a Pinhole of what is.

Beliefs dissolve the truth

We have already established that perception is not reality, so therefore, considering that a belief is created from our perception of something, it is also not a representative of reality.

A belief is just one version of one aspect of life, and no matter how closely it represents the truth, it is still just a version. In fact it would be reasonable to propose that to solidly believe in something obliterates any possibility we could ever have of actually experiencing it.

To illustrate my point lets look at the many different religions and beliefs in regard to the notion of there being a God that created all that we know. I do not want to debate whether there is or isn't a God, that is for you to decide or to know. But what I would like you to consider is, if you believe in God you have effectively disconnected any real possibility of there being a God. A belief is not real, therefore in your experiential reality you have just made God not real in your mind, hence God may still be there but you will never know it.

Fear narrows and distorts our thinking, and as beliefs are created from our fears, the best you can hope for is a distorted experience of what it is you believe in, including yourself!

We do not have to believe in something for it to exist, in fact when we do believe in it, it ceases to exist - as far as our experience is concerned.

So if we genuinely want to establish a connection with life or the possibility of there being a God, then I recommend that we stop believing in anything. To clarify, to believe in something is to simply create a cyber version of something, therefore we are not actually experiencing it, we are just experiencing it in the way our Problem-Solving Mind interprets it.

> **The only reason we believe in something is because we actually fear that it doesn't exist in the first place.**

Many people have said to me - I must believe in myself for my life to have meaning. If I don't believe in myself then what am I?

If you believe in yourself then effectively you have just limited your experience of being you to the confines of your mind's perception of you – which is again your life story. So at this point you will always feel dissatisfied because you are trying to be something that you are not.

This is why most people feel so confused and go on journeys to *find themselves*, thinking that if they dig deeper and more firmly into the their beliefs they will find the answers to what they seek. The further they travel blindly into their beliefs the more lost they will become, and the real them may never be experienced. So if one is to go on such a journey of discovery, remember to stay awake and realise that to experience beliefs is an opportunity to understand how the system that we are attempting to find peace in works. Resist the desire to reinforce them.

> **To really experience being you, stop believing in you and there you will be.**

Are you talking to me!

If you are comfortable with the concept that a belief is the only thing standing between you and the truth, then you will be able to see how strange it is that a belief is what we will fight for more than anything else on this planet.

Throughout human history wars have been created because of clashing beliefs; each side thinking they are right and that the other is wrong. The truth is both sides are wrong if you want to look at it from this angle. People collectively and individually continue to enforce their beliefs as if they are real, because they know no other reality despite the obvious outcomes of destructtion they create. Of course each side believes that if they are victorious, life will find a state of harmony; but of course it will not, as eventually another belief or set of beliefs will grow to create a new challenge for power and domination – and so on the saga goes. Victory over someone or something else does not change the fact that the victors are still trapped in their Construct - in fact, more deeply than they ever were before. To function along such a deluded pathway requires a level of denial and editing of life that negates any possibility of ever escaping the firm grip pain has on human existence. So as people are uniting in their beliefs and therefore their stories, they are uniting in their journey towards the pure essence of pain.

Beliefs are the foundations that underlie all of the rage and conflict that we witness in the behaviour of humanity.

> Effectively we are and always have been fighting over nothing!

The appearance of selfishness

The rather narrow, distorted and insubstantial angle from which the Problem-Solving Mind is attempting to approach life, creates the appearance of selfishness. Another key reason why it does not question this process of functioning is because the Problem-Solving Mind incorrectly believes that it is the most important thing in the Universe and that all of life revolves around it - hence the need to impose its perception onto the world. Therefore it does not think that it is selfish as it is just enforcing a truth that is fair and reasonable. However, our personal

Constructs (our individual life stories) are not the entirety of life, just one version of it.

The Problem-Solving Mind is constantly in a process of ensuring that survival of its existence is its primary motivator. Therefore it believes that it is absolutely necessary for it to manipulate the information that it receives and consequently presents to the world, in order to get what it wants.

Unfortunately or not, if we stay in this mode of functioning . . .

> All we will ever personally experience, and all that we will ever create on this planet, will be a distorted version of what is possible.

A chink in the armour

The Problem-Solving Mind is so unbelievably proficient at fulfilling the task that nature created it to do, that its functioning is almost foolproof. Hence it has been able to maintain its control over human existence throughout the history of our evolutionary pathway - leading us to the very era in which we currently exist.

But don't give up hope, because the operative words in the previous sentence that will set us free are:

Almost foolproof.

The Problem-Solving Mind is a very powerful piece of thinking machinery and it will take a lot of convincing for me to prove to it, which effectively means that I must prove to you, that you are not it. This may sound strange, but neither you nor it currently realise the true nature of this relationship, otherwise you would not be controlled by it!

Let me explain this a little further as this may sound hypocritical to what I have currently proposed. Yes it has taken ownership of us and it is in control of our existence, but it does not truly understand what it is and what we are, but to some degree it thinks it does. So as clever as it is, it has not been able to figure this out.

So now you may be asking; why can't it figure out what we are and what it is?

Because the Problem-Solving Mind can't see, touch, feel, smell and hear you or it – but it can use the body's senses to analyse the physical being that it is within, hence why it becomes so heavily identified with the physical body.

The Problem-Solving Mind is a representative of the physical realm and is therefore life looking at life. The reason it does not understand this is because it is still limiting itself to a distorted fear-based version – hence the creation of beliefs. As long as it continues to do this it will never clearly understand what it is.

There is only one force and energy that I am 'aware' of that can take the Problem-Solving Mind beyond its current self-limiting parameters, and that is Conscious Awareness.

It would appear to be quite obvious that the Problem-Solving Mind lacks one key ingredient within its own functioning and that is true awareness. It knows we are a source of energy that it can control and use for its own purpose, but it appears not to know that we are the very things that it needs to extend and expand the realm of its survival into the future – or does it?

Also stay open to the idea that the Problem-Solving Mind may be challenging us to wake up, as it is clear it will not let anything beyond its parameters that is not completely aware, awake and compassionate.

Every thought we have, every feeling we experience and all that we see humans create has been developed through the specific and focused thinking of our minds. We have become so heavily reliant upon these creations that to give them up and relinquish control seems almost ludicrous as a concept. The Problem-

PHASE EIGHT

Solving Mind presents to us that to do this would leave us with nothing as a replacement.

The end result is we get stuck living with the devil we know, rather than the falsely identified devil that we don't! To illustrate the power of 'the devil we know' look at this simple example of human denial created through the world of pain and beliefs.

I have known women who have young children, and they would take their children to the kiddie park at the zoo – where children get up close and personal with farm animals generally. One of the great attractions to mothers and their children are the baby lambs - not surprising really, as they are so adorable and cute, and mothers in general love all young things. Together mother and child would share the joy of spending time with other beautiful creatures.

All sounds pretty good so far.

Then on the way home they would visit more baby lambs together - this time dead ones chopped up into little pieces at the butcher shop. What do you think this is doing to the child's mind? Creating a desensitisation to life - confusion maybe?

This is not an uncommon story, but it does give you a glimpse of the distorted reality we exist in. Really think about this one - even a nurturing and caring woman could not make the connection between spending time with the lambs and eating them. In eating them, they as mothers are accepting that the baby lambs have been taken from their mothers and murdered.

If a mother, whilst immersed in the energy of love and giving, could not see the corruption in her actions, then imagine what else may be going on that we are not seeing.

It is quite funny to stop and think that murder is considered to be the most heinous of crimes, yet we sit down to eat murdered animals in their millions every day – and this we justify because our Construct of learning says *this* murder is alright. Can you see the danger in allowing our lives to be guided by such a system of thought?

Can an intelligent being really find an argument to justify this? Yet we do every day. Or even worse we don't even think about it. Now ask yourself what could possibly obscure such an obvious awareness in terms of distorted thinking? Well I hope you know the answer to this by now!

Looking at the *good* will never take away the *bad*. If we desire to see the whole truth behind what guides our lives, it is time to look at the parts of our behaviour that we conveniently ignore. How could we ever see this if we just keep looking at the aspects of life that we want to see?

Please also note that we have different levels of denial attached to different topics, as we still fight for those that we have acknowledged and associated with our life story. By enforcing life in such a fashion we just keep propelling the power of pain further forward into the creation of life.

It is essential that we learn to be compassionate in the entirety of what this energy represents. Not just when it is convenient and pertaining to our version of life. Otherwise we are still just enforcing and living within our Construct, rather than embracing all of life. Only Conscious Awareness can express itself with this level of purity because it can be no other way, and it is not limited by any perceptual reality. If you are Consciously Aware then you feel not just for yourself but also for all you encounter.

I am sharing awareness to create awareness; then we won't have to decide whether we are being cruel in our actions or not.

We will just know!

PHASE NINE

A global state of insanity

PHASE NINE

We know that so much of what we see and do and what we choose to ignore, is unacceptable within the realms of the truth that lies deep within us all.

Yet the madness continues because humanity is in denial of its role in the insanity.

Is humanity being sacrificed?

Pain is driving the processes of the Construct, which has been masterfully directed by the Problem-Solving Mind within every human being on this planet. The Insanity of Humanity is a by-product of this powerful combination, and it is often conveniently excused and disguised when the collective has created the necessary processes of justifications to deflect individual responsibility.

> **Hence we are collectively creating a world that we are struggling to live in, as if we did not build it.**

So let's have a look at what can happen when a planet is essentially infected by billions of a highly intelligent species that are allowing their lives to be guided by pain. We will explore the ramifications of this global reality that we are all witnessing, to guide us on our journey of awareness. On this journey, we will have the opportunity to enable ourselves to function beyond the insanity that is consuming large portions of the human genus. Once we create some honesty as to our existing global reality, we can then look more closely and honestly at the nature of the Construct and the Problem-Solving Mind.

What was nature thinking, creating all of this pain and suffering and channelling it through the processes of the Problem-Solving Mind, which ultimately brings all of this suffering into our lives?

It brings not only suffering into our lives but also massive levels of stupidity, relative to the human mind's potential. Particularly when we consider that we spend more time using our intelligence to look for something to blame for our pain, rather than understanding the processes that are causing it.

Maybe there is method in this madness that we as a collective species just can't see yet. On the whole, we can't. The current pathway we are on keeps us in a state of blindness, as it powerfully serves something far greater than you or me as individuals.

Think about how many people you know that feel life is somehow unfair and that it does not have their best interests in mind.

Well as things currently stand, they are right!

This observation is clearly reflected in the functioning of all societies worldwide, whereby the lives of individual humans and animals are happily sacrificed for the *greater cause* of humanity. As much as this approach creates a false sense of security, we all know that any of us could be targeted just by being in the wrong place at the wrong time.

You could be next!

I find it intriguing that we as a species could ever buy into this notion of selectively justifying sacrifice as being acceptable and justifiable, let alone the brutality that is used in the process of enforcing it. There is quite obviously a flaw in this mode of thinking if we are to create a world where we genuinely want people to care about each other. How could we ever possibly hope to achieve peace and harmony, when we have empowered ourselves to conveniently decide when life is expendable or not, based on circumstances, desired outcomes, our learning and our beliefs.

If one is to be totally honest and wants to function from a place of integrity, then calculated destruction is never okay, and there is no cause great enough to justify the sacrifice of anything; unless of course the corruption of the human spirit is acceptable to us. But pain has an amazing ability to allow us to see what is convenient rather than absorbing the truth of our behaviour.

Really consider what I am saying here.

A global state of insanity

If we continue to empower ourselves with the ability to place a value on different forms of life, or each other, then we are never going to get to a place where we value life as a whole.

One would think the treatment of people during the Second World War was evidence enough – proof of the danger and destruction that occurs when beliefs guide our value systems. So instead of waking up to the truth embodied in these experiences, humanity has decided that certain evil people were responsible, rather than facing that this type of behaviour is waiting to be created within all of us. All it takes is the right conditioning driven by a cleverly crafted story of fear. We have done it again in the Middle East, as many innocent women, men, children and animals have been killed for some greater cause. It is time to learn, to grow and to become aware!

Although these are extreme human examples, do you think that for non-human animals to be caged in torturous conditions as we manipulate their lives towards their ultimate demise for our own pleasure and survival is acceptable? If people were being honest the answer would have to be yes - as this is happening right now as we read, sleep, eat and go about our daily lives. On the whole we are doing little to change this. In Australia, the cruelty to caged hens has been recognised openly, yet people continue to buy the eggs from creatures that they know are suffering. The governments of the day, under some social pressure from various animal rights organisations, create long term plans to stop this - yes, long term!

How do we *wean out* cruelty once recognised?

Surely we would just stop it immediately! Once again we are justifying sacrifice for the almighty dollar. The leaders that dictate our future never talk of such issues because they are unaware of them in a real sense; in terms of what it is that guides their thinking and their denial in the first place.

So the point to truly consider is:

If we can justify the cruelty inflicted upon a chicken, we can justify the cruelty to anything - including human beings!

Once we wake up to a place of united Conscious Awareness, then we won't have to decide what to value, as cruelty would be unacceptable to all. If we can feel compassion for ourselves, then we obviously have the ability to feel compassion for everyone and everything - and until we do, our future is debateable.

If we survive as a species then no one will have to fight for their rights and no one will eat or kill animals. We could live no other way and still live with ourselves, as harming others is the same as harming ourselves.

Think about people throughout history that have fought so hard to be valued equally with others - whether they are woman in general, the Australian Aborigines or African Americans. Yet can these same people broaden this awareness beyond their own rights, to a place of compassion for all living creatures? The truthful answer is quite often no, they cannot! They get acknowledgement of their rights but still seem incapable of broadening this awareness to value all of life.

As things stand, when human thought is being controlled by pain, we often do not take our learning beyond our own personal experiences, and so we fight for segregated causes without shining the same light of integrity on ourselves. Once again this is evidence that we are lost in our life story, a very narrow existence, a pathway that disallows us from seeing the entirety of life. This means we are only experiencing a small portion of ourselves, hence the intensified pain that allows us to make decisions that encompass the suffering of others.

The true test of human character is in how we behave towards those things

that we *don't have to* treat with decency, compassion and respect.

If we as a species cannot create a united mode of awareness, that has the underlying property of respect for all of life, then there will always be something that we need badly enough that will justify the sacrifice of something else to get what we want. As I said, how do you feel when this very process of thinking that we are currently justifying turns on you? Does it still seem fair, reasonable and appropriate, or is it suddenly a moment of injustice because you are now the target?

One could argue this approach, whereby we justify sacrifice for gain, is necessary for the continuance of progress; however, what sort of world are we going to be happy to live in? Is being alive that precious that we will do anything to hold on to it, even though inevitably it is going to end whether we like it or not? Do you get a little hint of insanity in that?

We have become so obsessed with staying alive that we don't know how to live.

So given humanity is quite obviously struggling to work out how to create peaceful and harmonious civilisations, how could it be that we actually think we are intelligent or wise enough to be able to place a value system on life itself?

How do we value something we don't even understand?

It is our beliefs that are guiding the processes within ourselves, or within our leaders that pick and choose when sacrifice is acceptable.

All beliefs are corruptible because they are fear-based mechanisms, and they only have survival of the physical being as their primary goal. When using beliefs to guide our lives we are not interested in the entirety of life, but only in the small segments pertaining to our notion of existence. Therefore, to use a belief to guide the processes of valuing life and the proceeding choices of sacrifice is fraught with potential corruption. This is exactly what is happening in the world today. This programmed blind selfishness that we must all live with, does perfectly serve the processes of what we have defined as evolution.

The interesting part of all this is; as people continue to empower themselves with decision-making that is actually beyond their existing realm of awareness, they inadvertently keep themselves trapped at a certain level of existence, owing to the confusion that this creates. Meaning, they are playing a game where they don't even really understand the rules. Therefore the outcomes are always totally confusing and the world continues to be seen as a problem. So the rules of life become an elusive thing that we shall never understand, hence the empowerment of the Problem-Solving Mind and the continuance of our incarceration within the Construct.

So it would be reasonable to propose that it is in fact humanity that is unwittingly offering itself as the sacrificial lamb.

If we continue to empower ourselves with the ability to place value and controls upon something that we do not understand, then the truth shall never be ours to see. The processes of thinking required to value other entities' lives as less than our own are the same processes that are creating the pathways towards the psychological black hole of our minds.

In sacrificing other life forms we are inadvertently sacrificing ourselves.

The old saying 'you can't have your cake and eat it too' is definitely true. We can't justify cruelty and think we can get away with it, just because the majority of people in our chosen place of residence condone it. We may be able to avoid external judgement, but we will be punished in other ways I assure you.

A global state of insanity

Every time we find a way to conveniently accept the unacceptable, the strength and nature of the enforcement in our mental prison is increasing!

See these pathways of denial and justifications as control; control that we think is necessary because we continue to see life as a problem that needs solving. The completely ridiculous part of all this, is that life does not need to be conquered. Humanity is trying to solve something that does not want to be solved and that can only lead to increased levels of disharmony and pain.

We are the experience, so when we attack and destroy the experience we are doing the same to ourselves!

Life is what it is, and it is time for us to learn to flow with it, but first we must learn to understand it. We will never understand it if we don't open our eyes beyond our programmed needs to feel good.

Until this point in time, we thought we were gaining personal and global power by controlling, analysing and experimenting with life. But we have made one fatal mistake; gaining control has no limits or boundaries. It is an insatiable desire because control does not actually take fear away. It increases it as we become scared of losing the security we have acquired. By following this route we have forced our fears onto life, rather than guiding its journey with integrity and wisdom.

Now we are all paying the price for our lack of patience!

If it wasn't pain and fear that was driving us we would be much wiser by now, because we would have spent more time sensing the true nature of life as opposed to foolishly trying to control it. So here we are still trying to take pride in our technology and our progress, constantly justifying what we have done to gain this knowledge and desperately needing to tell ourselves how special we are. It is as if humanity is trying to prove itself, in some vain attempt to gain recognition for its dominance and superiority over other living things. But from whom do we want recognition?

> What kind of entity would respect and applaud achievement that has an ugly trail of blood behind it?

The deep insecurities that drive this process are what allow for the highly immoral behaviour from which humanity reaps its falsely identified rewards. Of course, we are finding out very quickly that the rewards coming from control, particularly through this phase of rapid technological advancement, are in fact an elusive lure that is only offering a false promise of happiness.

We are all behaving like scared little children that desperately need to have our *wants* satisfied and desperately need to feel secure to be happy. Do not see this as a condemnation of humanity - open your eyes instead. See that this modern-day phenomenon of advanced levels of physical and psychological destruction is exposing the true nature and functioning of the inside of the human mind when guided by misunderstood pain.

Corruption

As the Problem-Solving Mind is gaining greater control over the functioning of humanity, we are witnessing higher levels of corruption. The potentially alarming part of this observation is that for quite a long time leading up to the present day, governments and businesses have made quite extreme attempts to disguise any type of deceptive or manipulative behaviour. However, it has become apparent very recently that individuals representing us in positions of power are blatantly and arrogantly throwing down their masks, confidently exposing the true nature of their fraudulent behaviour.

In examining this modern-day phenomenon, it is very important to observe the way people behave when commonly shared beliefs are under strain. This encourages people to unite when they would normally be living a life of segregation. This allows for extraordinarily high levels of corruption as individual responsibility is conveniently disguised by a so-called greater cause. This leaves people prepared to behave in a manner they may have otherwise faced and found unacceptable. So as individuals are hiding from facing the truth of their own behaviour, they not only become more corruptible but also easier to control as their levels of fear are higher and therefore their need to be guided towards security increases.

At times of global uncertainty, security becomes the primary focus. What we are prepared to do to gain this security stretches the boundaries of anyone's definition of integrity.

So hopefully you are starting to get some sense that corruption is a malleable reality, which shifts and changes to suit the purposes of satisfying human need, via the pathways of the Problem-Solving Mind. If you would like to get a clearer idea of what I'm talking about, then look through the history of the human species within one particular culture, preferably your own. Then take note of how, what is considered to be tolerable behaviour, changes depending on the era.

Note that different eras simply represent differently programmed Constructs, but don't be fooled by this, for Constructs create many faces to disguise their systematic and predictable behind-the-scenes processes of functioning.

To illustrate this point let's take a look at another time in the history of human evolution.

She is a witch!

Let's journey to Salem, Massachusetts in the spring of 1692.

PHASE NINE

You've just been accused of being a witch. The reason for the accusation against you might have arisen from a long list of possibilities. Perhaps you talk to yourself, you're reclusive, or exhibit some other form of eccentric behaviour.

Sound familiar?

Perhaps you don't go to church, or go to the wrong church. Perhaps you speak French! Or perhaps you expressed support for a recently accused witch, or worse yet, accused the accusers of lying. Whatever the reason, you're situation is not looking promising.

So what are your options?

- Confess to avoid death and let God deal with you.
- Get pregnant and face trial once the baby is born.
- Plead innocent and stand for trial.
- Refuse to stand for trial – but be mindful that one woman who refused to plead to the charges was pressed to death with rocks.

Whatever option you choose is not looking good for you. Why? Because the Construct of that era (like all Constructs) was created from fear. Fear of what is not understood is controlled.

It was a Construct of thinking that led to the process of irrational behaviour that allowed for the justification of the destruction of innocent people's lives in Salem in 1692.

So do you think that the activities and things that we accept today are not also full of such obscene justifications? I assure you they are. It is only when we are housed in the Construct that we will not allow ourselves to see the truth of the consequences of our own behaviour, or that of society as a whole. We have only rearranged the bits and pieces of the puzzle to create the same scenario in a different disguise. If we were all to take an honest look at the very systems that we are partaking in and contributing

A global state of insanity

to, by the very nature of accepting them, then I assure you, if integrity was our guide, we would have to change many aspects of our lives quite dramatically.

Would you be prepared to do that? Well, some of you might say yes, but our Problem-Solving Mind would not allow the majority of us to do so for this would contravene its intention of maintaining control.

Fear has led us into a state of functioning where we believe that being in control is more important than living with integrity.

Can you sit comfortably with yourself and say that this is okay?

Whatever your answer is, if we do not face the truth of what I am presenting then our lives will continue to be one of dissatisfaction and confusion, as we unite in denial towards our demise. This is why it is so important to explore, not only our individual behaviour, but also the global reality that is dramatically influencing our behaviour without us even realising it.

We are uniting in a constant process of shared information and that information is becoming embodied with increasing levels of pain and fear.

Given that we know that fear corrupts behaviour, it is not hard to imagine where this is leading us. The more we feel fear the more we share fear. The more we share it, the more we feel the need to control life to protect ourselves. The more we control life in general, the more we become individually controlled, and therefore our levels of fear and pain increase, and so on it goes. Embodied in this process is also the exponential growth of the justification for corruption and cruelty, as fear makes us blind to caring about things outside of our own survival.

Also please note that as this fear is spreading rampantly across the planet from one individual to another, it is taking all of us further and further away from the truth of where our freedom lies. For our freedom will never be found from continually protecting ourselves against our perceived enemy. It will only be found when we wake up to the reality that we are living inside the Construct, an interactive cyber reality that has consumed the human spirit. Once again, let me reiterate that this is the Insanity of Humanity.

Humanity is destroying life to maintain life for the fear of facing life!

Yet on we go from generation to generation functioning the same way. In fact, worse than that, we are actually building and reinforcing the very machinery that creates it.

Of course denial of what I am presenting has been conveniently argued and debated for many centuries, because one group of united Constructs think they know better than another group. Therefore it is the *others* that are ruining everything, so we justify violence and sacrifice to resolve clashes in beliefs. This will go on forever because none of them is the truth, and therefore it doesn't matter who wins and takes control, humanity will always be guided towards the same place; a dark and ugly misguided world.

So even though it may look like our eternal thinking and analysis of life is leading us towards being in control of our environment, and of other people whose beliefs are in conflict with our own, the truth is far removed from how we conveniently perceive it.

We are going to destroy life all around us in order to protect ourselves, because our beliefs tell us that this is what we should do. Do you think humanity will one day look back and acknowledge how we live today as being foolish, primitive, cruel and selfish? How we were able to conveniently justify the sacrifice of other living things to get what we wanted, to get control?

Well I hope the answer to this question is yes!

Because if it is yes, it means that we realised this entire dilemma and united together in the sharing of wisdom, instead of partaking in the divisiveness that misunderstood pain continues to create.

And if the answer is yes then lets act on this now and build that world!

I cannot underestimate how important it is for all of us to see the larger more lateral picture before we can truly move on to finding individual freedom. Interestingly, once one finds this personal freedom, life no longer feels like you are an individual in an isolated sense, but rather part of a united process of life.

Trading integrity for control

Without integrity, what are we?

Without integrity nobody can trust anybody, and we will continue to live in a world where we're trapped in the game of deceit and manipulation, The Game of the Construct - a game where we justify and accept the most obscene realities in order to protect our fears and maintain control.

Can you see that this technique is simply not working?

The more we as individuals go down this pathway, the more we create a uniting of minds all trapped in the same mode of functioning - creating a world that we are finding difficult to live in.

We are doing this to ourselves!

Even if you were to be the only person on the planet that could wake up to the truth, break free from the insanity and start to live a life with genuine awareness and integrity, then do it, because at least you will be able to die with dignity.

You will be able to die alive!

If we were to actually shine the light of truth on all of us, then we would all have to be thrown in jail.

'How ridiculous,' I hear in the background, well surprise surprise!

Because inadvertently that is exactly what has happened to all of us, as we are all in a place of incarceration. Maybe this is universal karma and planet Earth has been reserved for us less than honest ones!

Or maybe life on Earth is simply the testing ground where only those with deep integrity can pull out of the corruption, and therefore earn the right to continue the journey of life into eternity.

Remember that to feel incarcerated is in fact just that . . . a feeling!

It is a feeling that is derived from a certain type of thinking. It is our current mode of thinking, whereby we are connected to our belief structures, that is creating the forever-decreasing boundaries of our existence. This is because our beliefs of what we should fear are increasing. Therefore the bars of our interconnected cage are becoming thicker and harder to see through.

I assure you that the truth lies outside of the cage.

Now as this process makes our personal world feel smaller the dynamics of control are getting bigger. This leads to higher levels of corruption, meaning that the system and laws of functioning that guide us, contain less morality and integrity as time goes on.

This is the perfect scenario for governments to take control of the individual. For if the individual feels overwhelmed most of the time, then the last thing they are going to put their energy into is questioning their own behaviour within the parameters of the law, whether it is founded with integrity or not.

Perfect! Give the creator of that one a gold star for excellence in manipulation.

A global state of insanity

The human mind is affected by learning more than the mind of any other creature on this planet, and therefore it also has far less innate programs than any other creature. This gives our minds more flexibility in terms of the possibilities of how we function and adapt to different environments. It is a great survival mechanism for creative problem-solving, but now without question it is working against us. This is because it also leaves us extremely open to being manipulated and controlled, to the point where we are unaware of the consequences of our own behaviour. This collective manipulation of our minds on a global scale is creating such divisiveness, that it is getting to the point that no one really has a clue what they're doing any more.

Humanity is fighting humanity so therefore no matter who wins we all lose!

As long as we live in the world of beliefs then we will always think it is other humans we must protect ourselves against. Once again this process of thinking perfectly services the functioning of the Construct, as we battle against our falsely identified enemy, which is in fact just us fighting us.

We may as well just go into a room and individually beat ourselves up, as that would encompass the same level of sanity as the processes that we are currently consumed by.

Well I have some bad news for you – essentially we are already doing this too.

Tell me one person that you know who does not question themselves and beat themselves up intellectually and emotionally over the wrongs and rights of the choices they have made in their past? Of course, this is just an eternal and never-ending battle with no right answer, so we jump right back onto the boat of blaming others!

Before we will ever get the chance to experience a more highly developed process of functioning, we must first understand the ramifications of what pain is causing in today's world. Otherwise we will never make the necessary moves to change our ways. Currently we have become totally addicted to and reliant upon the systems that pain has created. These systems are therefore immobilising our ability to let go of our fear, even though it is our systems of functioning that are forcing the sensation of fear to levels that are crippling all of humanity. This will only serve to create a life whereby we will be continually swapping between the processes of control and compromise - a behaviour that leads to nothing but futile and primitive power struggles with other people.

PHASE TEN

Pain collection machines

Global amassing of pain

Pain and the fear it creates can spread from one individual to another very rapidly, and with the advent of today's technology this process has been greatly accelerated to create a global phenomenon.

Many aspects to the global amassing of pain are worth considering. This will help create an understanding of your own functioning and whether you want to continue to contribute to this process or not. To cover every aspect of how pain accumulates globally would require a book devoted to this topic, as it is a big one with very complex interwoven realities attached. So for now let's just have a look at some of the key issues that will help you create the necessary foundation for the development of your awareness.

Firstly, within your lifetime, whatever age you are, you have probably grown up in a system which functions through a process of control, which uses fear to achieve its objectives. Ask yourself a simple question to explore what I am saying. How does the functioning of the system you live in determine the nature of how you are able to express your existence - with respect and intelligent wisdom, or with the threat of reprisal?

Despite the sometimes rather soft and fluffy disguises that it hides behind, the message of threat and reprisal is the norm; which in essence means the use or threat of physical violence to enforce one's will upon another. Let me share a real life and personal experience to reflect this reality.

She screamed for help but nobody responded

And her screams were certainly not unfounded.

Pain collection machines

I was walking home from a restaurant one night towards our car with my partner and a female friend. Little did we know what experience was to follow!

I momentarily stopped in a state of disbelief.

My friends and I witnessed a brutal assault of a man being held down by four young uniformed policemen. I did not know the man whom they were assaulting, or what he had done, but what was clear, was that he was unconscious as the brutality continued. So I quickly scanned the area to look for another policeman and asked him to stop the violence.

I did not quite get the response that I was looking for.

I was told to "F - off" in no uncertain terms. So I asked again. He then proceeded to bash me in the chest with his fists and continued to swear at me. I challenged his violent behaviour by questioning the integrity of his actions. Yes, perhaps a little stupid on my part, as the next response was inevitable. So in the horror of what little I could do to help this man from being beaten, by those that are supposedly there to serve and protect us, I was forced to exit the area.

At this point, I realised that I had been separated from my friends. We eventually made eye contact from a distance and then motioned to each other to stay right where we were until things settled down. Finally, the police were allowing people to freely walk down the footpath. My friends and I proceeded to walk towards each other and this is where the story gets interesting . . .

The young policemen that had taken a rather strong disliking to my presence, walked up to me, shoved me in the chest again and said, "I told you to F – off." I explained to him that the two women behind him were my friends and that our car was literally 10 metres away, and that we needed to go in that direction to go home. I don't think rational thinking was the energy of the moment. He continued to physically and verbally attack me. So I asked for his badge number and his name to no avail.

PHASE TEN

The next unexpected turn in this event was the entry of a man that I presumed was a detective. He started to question me as to what was going on. I felt an absolute sense of relief that finally an opportunity to be heard had arisen.

He cut me off halfway through my story and said, "Why the F should I listen to you?" I was a little dumbfounded by the response, but at least I knew what their favourite word was! Next I was pulled from behind by the uniformed policeman and thrown across the pavement.

Before I knew it, I had five police pulling at me from every angle. All I could think was that I did not want to be taken to the ground after what I had recently witnessed. My friends were screaming at them to stop and all they received was transference of the aggression towards them.

It wasn't long before the force of what was upon me weighed me down and I remember falling backwards towards the concrete. Once I hit the ground they all leapt on me and proceeded to punch me and bend my limbs in angles they were certainly not designed to go. As this was happening, I was appealing for some deeper sense of reasoning within them. So in response to this, as the men held me down, a female police officer proceeded to lean forward and punch me in the face. As if this was not enough, I was rolled onto my front, my head was pulled backwards from my hair and my forehead was slammed into the concrete footpath.

I was then handcuffed, verbally threatened and thrown into the back of a police wagon. I sat in the wagon trying to figure out how this could all be possible. One moment I was trying to help another fellow human being and then the next I was the one being attacked.

Eventually my friends found their way to the police station that I was transported to and they insisted I be released. My friends just wanted to give statements in my defence, however, they were told to get lost and go home.

Pain collection machines

Fortunately for me, my friends never ceased in their demands for my release, and after I was subjected to many hours of ongoing verbal abuse and humiliation, I was set free from their controls.

I ended up with many bruises, badly damaged joints, a damaged spine and a broken rib. For quite a long time after, I genuinely felt that I had no feeling of trust for the very system that I was bound into. I felt the strong need to fight it and to right a wrong.

I had to ask myself, what was I fighting against? What does fighting achieve anyway? Does it not just reinforce the resolve of the thing you are fighting against?

The individuals that assaulted me were not the whole issue; they were just young people with power that exceeded their levels of maturity, awareness and wisdom. The governments that utilise and give power to the police are not the whole issue - the issue is all of us. We all allow it to be this way. Why? Because we live in a world that is driven by pain and fear.

The main point to absorb here is that as long as violence is used as the main technique for maintaining control, then emotional repression will increase as the controls and laws spread wider into the far reaches of our minds.

So whether you like it or not, or whether you are even aware of it, more than likely you are living in a permanent state of repression, which is therefore, even if extremely subtle, a permanent state of fear. The pain-based energy in an environment like ours, spreads from one individual to another, infecting anyone that enters this arena. Our repression literally creates a mass entity of fear and pain that is comprised of the accumulation of the individuals within it.

It is the processes of control that keep this mass entity together as a united force of pain. Every single aspect of the systems and structures that we currently live in has been built through the processes of our Problem-Solving Minds, and guided by pain and the fear that it manifests. Therefore, our societies are the physical representation of the functioning of the Problem-Solving Mind. I will explain this a little further. Remember that the mind is confused how to clearly get in touch with the world it experiences, and therefore the closest thing that it can create to a physical structure within itself is a belief. So then the mind tries to bring this belief to life by using the human body to create external structures and systems of functioning that match its internal world of beliefs.

Also it is worth paying further attention to the fact that all of the leaders of the systems that the Problem-Solving Mind has created are also just a representative of its functioning. The leaders that emerge are those of us whose personality structures, learning and brain functioning most closely fit into the systems we have all created.

Don't waste your time getting angry with the leaders that you see guiding the destiny of humanity, because they are only the representatives of what we have all created. They are those of us whose Conscious Energy is most removed from transforming into a state of awareness.

So if you think it is time for a different kind of leader, then it is time to create different systems of life for us to express ourselves within. We can only do this by changing the functioning of each and every individual person, until the majority learn to function beyond the parameters of the Construct.

Don't underestimate what I am proposing here, as we are all more deeply entrenched in our psychological cages than we realise.

Fear corrupts and creates irrational behaviour; we can see that within anybody. What we don't realise, is that we are all permanently living in and being guided by, at the very least, subtle levels of the energy that embodies fear. Therefore humanity just continues to forge forward in this direction of corruption and control, as if this pathway could somehow ever lead to a place of peace and harmony. It is as if we keep thinking the answers and solutions we are looking for are always just

Pain collection machines

around the next corner - an illusionary corner that is just a false notion in our minds that we never actually arrive at.

It is not hard to imagine, once you embrace the awareness of what I am presenting, how pain grows and accumulates an overwhelming amount of power over the group and over the individuals within it. Then as the system controls the group, the individuals within it create their own little groups. They do this in an attempt to get their own version of power as they try to take back what has been taken away from them and so on it goes.

> **If there is any element of control attached to your life, then something is being taken away from you otherwise there would no be no need for control.**

Nobody feels good being controlled or having to give up part of the functioning of his or her mental structure. This simply fuels the power of pain and this pain must be channelled back into something. Some people may try and control their employees, some may try and control their partners, and others may channel their fear and pain by controlling their pets, the weak or the disadvantaged. I am sure we all remember the bullies at school.

> **The only reason we attempt to control other things is to make our own life feel like it's under control.**

Sometimes people disguise their pain and need to control within 'good' causes. Not ever recognising that channelling pain in any direction, other than for the purpose of gathering wisdom, is buying into the never-ending loop of insanity. Whatever the scenario, I am painting a picture to help you see that fear and pain keep transferring from one living thing to another. If you want it to stop, then you must first become aware that it is happening and become aware of your part in this game.

PHASE TEN

We only feel psychological pain when we perceive something to have been taken away from us, and this is how we justify our processes of using control to get something back.

But for us to get something back means that we to have to take something away from someone or something else - hence the continuance of this insane process.

This energy space that we are all living in, which is the energy that unites all Constructs, affects every piece of information we receive, communicate and share with each other. It therefore has a massive effect on the belief structures we create about the world we live in. This affects the process of how our mind filters information that is presented to us, which unintentionally on our part, affects our behaviour.

Even though it is not you directly that is creating the mayhem, you do have the power and ability to change these processes of functioning. You have the ability to become aware!

It would appear the larger proportion of the human population does not know the truth behind what is guiding their behaviour. It is no surprise that we are observing increasing levels of fear, increasing levels of psychological disturbance, increasing levels of destructive behaviour, and therefore increasing levels of control to maintain and guide this fear by the very systems that are supposedly there to protect us. The only reason that governments are able to convincingly sell to us that control is in our interest is because we have already bought in to the belief that this is true. Even though we are all feeling the repression of being controlled, somehow we think the benefits outweigh the costs because our lives will be safer. Given this is an ongoing cycle that grows exponentially, try and imagine where this is leading us. As the controls in society increase, the parameters of our freedom to move and make choices within our incarceration decrease.

Pain collection machines

We are being moved slowly but surely down a corridor from one level of a high security prison to the next, where our privileges decrease and the rules controlling our behaviour increase.

How could we possibly see this as being in our best interest?

We are creating this world. It will continue until we are all effectively living in a tiny and tight little world. Remember that life for you is occurring on the inside of your mind; so if your mind's parameters get smaller and smaller, the sensation of your life will also get proportionately smaller.

We are being sold control for the protection of our freedom and rights as individuals, yet our freedom of emotional expression is what is being taken away from us.

The global amassing of pain and fear has led us to trade our freedom for a falsely identified security.

So why would we do this to ourselves?

Because we are feeling so psychologically weak and insecure, therefore we feel more in control within the notion of security.

We have not within our society developed the ability and skills to learn how to utilise our freedom effectively. When the levels of fear in society get great enough, we filter out all information other than that which is perceived as a threat, which is the stage we are at now. This obviously leaves us in such a vulnerable state that the offer of control and security seems like a gift from the heavens. However, I assure you that the face behind the giver of such illusionary good fortune is very different from the one that we are being presented with. Don't be fooled by the smile behind the offer of security, for you are being lured into the black hole of your mind!

People are in so much fear they get stuck in a permanent state of alertness to danger as their minds try to protect themselves from the pain. Unfortunately, this will leave them experiencing nothing but pain and a more desperate and insecure need for happiness. If this is how you feel a lot of the time, then this is who you will think you are – a person that is not easy to like, or be comfortable with, whether by you or by other people.

The result is that we keep empowering the need for the justifications of our social masks, which continue to lead to the very systems that we complain about and the very behaviour we despise. Yet, our Problem-Solving Minds would never allow us to believe that *we* are the problem, so our attention permanently gets diverted to everything that is perceived to be outside of us. The end result is we have many billions of people on the planet collectively thinking that life's problems lie somewhere outside of their own mind, even though they know the pain is in their mind. This is why the Super Construct can continue its reign of control over the human race.

It's a strange thought isn't it? To think that individually we are all going to suffer because of the systems that we are building, and yet somehow continuing to develop. Something is influencing humanity that is beyond our current state of awareness. So for this to change, we must all collectively start focusing our attention onto the reality that we are actually trapped within self-created illusionary parameters. Otherwise, the systems of control will continue and our lives will proceed to feel progressively less significant, until we end up as faceless creatures trapped inside our own technology.

To clarify; the more pain we feel the worse we behave, then the worse we behave the more justifications governments have to increase their levels of control over us. This leads to more fear and repression of individual emotional expression, which makes us feel more vulnerable and out of control. We therefore become more open to the possibilities of corruption in our own behaviour, which inadvertently leaves us open to being taken

Pain collection machines

advantage of by others. This is because our needs have become corrupted with fear and therefore are not representing the true essence of what we are. They are leading us down an insatiable and elusive pathway. This leaves us all in a state of deep insecurity while attempting to put forward a social mask of confidence . . . this is exhausting.

But don't jump onto the victim platform too quickly, expounding your disgust that this could possibly be happening to you. We are all partaking in the same process and therefore we are all responsible for what we are experiencing.

We will continue to play the role of victim in all of its many justifiable disguises, until we realise we are living in a purpose-built cyber program of functioning.

The Construct requires us to unite to create a system that could function in such a manner. If you do not like the picture I have painted, then start by individually removing yourself from the processes of pain you have become so deeply reliant upon. As hard as this is to do, the starting point is to simply shine the light of awareness on this reality. Allow your Consciousness to become aware in the entirety of its existence, which means no denial or avoidance of anything!

This certainly points to an interesting characteristic of living within the Construct; its ability to create such masterful illusions within its interactive game of deception, which we aren't even aware we are playing. We therefore think this mode of functioning is normal and therefore this allows for the uniting of individual Constructs. This inevitably creates the overall systems of functioning that are controlling us, yet these systems could not exist without all of us individually feeding this cyber realm.

Because we are all trapped in the same place we continue to justify so much of what we know is wrong and that is because we know no other way to function. This leaves us with only one choice, and that is to live in denial of the pain and suffering that our footprint is creating on this planet.

Humanity's footprint is a visual image of pain.

Good versus evil

If you really want to open your mind to the possibilities of the truth behind the systems of functioning that you are trapped in, then try to see the manifestation of everything you are witnessing as one entity. The system of functioning that is creating the falsely identified 'white knights' – the *saviours of humanity*, is the same system that is creating the falsely identified 'evil' – the *terrorist*, which these 'good guys' are attempting to destroy.

There is no good and there is no evil within the realms we are currently experiencing, it is all one thing. Let's explore this concept of good and evil a little further. It is becoming an ever increasing and prominent concept throughout the development and evolution of our global state of insanity.

The potentially destructive pathways that pain can manifest through the processes of the human mind, creates the falsely identified battle between good and evil. The abrasive effects are created when different belief structures block each other's desire for control. The ridiculous aspect to this process is each side thinks they are good and the other is evil. Take note when you watch the news in future, how often our world leaders talk about the evil they must control and destroy, as if somehow they are functioning from a place of purity and integrity. They say this because they think this is what we want to hear.

If we keep fighting each other behind the disguise of accumulated belief structures, we will never truly face the responsibility of the pain that we feel and the corruption in our own behaviour. We will therefore continue down a path of blaming and destroying. If we do not take stock of the pain that we experience as an individual, we will proceed to create a

Pain collection machines

collective human pathway that will lead to the extermination of our civilisations.

If we are able to individually free ourselves from the pathways of pain, then it will be very easy for us to step back and see what is there for all to see right now. I know this is the last thing any person wants to hear. This is because they have fully bought into the notion that the only way we will ever find peace and security in the future, is if we destroy the evil that is taking our freedom away. However, there is no evil taking our freedom away, at least not in the manner we are currently perceiving it.

The Construct and the Problem-Solving Mind are controlling and manufacturing all individual human behaviour, therefore they are also creating the supposed evil and the supposed good, and this is part of The Game. They are all just cyber realities that perfectly serve the purpose of evolution.

We are all creating this evil that we are fighting against.

The concept that control is a technique that is working has been enhanced because governments worldwide have united on the pathway to destroy the evil they have identified. The group mentality has gone to a new extreme! The more we increase the levels of control against an opposing force, the more the undesirable parameters of the things we are supposedly fighting against grow in intensity. Eventually these parameters become too great to handle and everyone will feel the psychological consequences on an individual basis. The leaders of the various countries can only keep justifying their methods of destruction to gain control, because we are all allowing them do it.

The people have the numbers and without the people governments have no power whatsoever.

If we are united in insanity then our world will be a representative of insanity, and if we are

united in wisdom then our world will be a representative of wisdom.

These processes of control create a never ending and futile pathway that has been tried endlessly throughout the history of humanity. However, they are still very tempting because they offer a quick-fix solution to appease the Problem-Solving Mind's insatiable need for security.

It is time for humanity to pull together and realise we are all trapped in the Construct and we can all unite in our awareness of this, therefore leading us to the realisation that no one is to blame specifically.

Together we can free ourselves from this psychological place of incarceration.

Remember the only way we can get control is ultimately through a process of physical intimidation, which means the threat of pain or death. Any acts of violence or control towards one individual from another, or from one country to another, can only be sourced by great pain. We must learn to understand this pain, because our ability to make wise decisions is being obscured by the fear it creates.

If you feel determined to look for 'evil' then start by looking for it within your own mind and within your own culture, because you are creating the Construct that is making your life feel so tight and fearful. We are all allowing our governments to lure us down a pathway where security is the answer to everything.

You may not individually be able to stand up against the whole system, but you can individually free yourself from the incarceration within your own mind. This can only happen when you stop accepting the human and non-human animal suffering that is all around you.

When you get to this point you will stop believing in what the system is telling you and you will start finding the truth through a process of integrity and wisdom. At the very least, you will enjoy the freedom and sense of purity that comes from functioning beyond your fear based beliefs.

Humanity will need to stop using external power as a means to an end, or an end is all we will have.

PHASE ELEVEN

The Information Super-Highway

PHASE ELEVEN

Is information power?

Information certainly is power, but the question to be asking ourselves is:

Power to do what and by whom?

Human beings are information-transference machines. We are constantly receiving, editing and spreading information from mind to mind. Technology is speeding up this process to a swiftness that can allow for rapid social reprogramming.

To gather some perspective, let's travel back in time for a moment to compare this to our more primitive ancestors.

There was a time when we did not have any sophisticated form of language at all, and therefore to even communicate from one person to another would have been somewhat difficult, let alone communicating to a whole group. The information that was shared would have rarely spread outside of the group, and so progressive change was slow as learning was slow. Since these primitive times, the need to survive forced the need to improve the pathways of communication from one person to another and from one location to another.

This process has greatly accelerated in the last century, which has led to the creation of the Information Super-Highway.

With the advent of digital technology and its application to various modes of communication such as mobile phones and the Internet, we now have access to information at our fingertips. So yes, information certainly creates power, but it has up until quite recently, primarily been used to enhance the processes of manipulation and control. However, the latest technological advances have also had a somewhat unexpected outcome. People are being linked and united in a way they never have before. These individuals are therefore having a great impact on the direction of how we think and on the future of business.

The Information Super Highway

Businesses more than ever are trying to go with the flow of human thinking, as they have to relinquish an element of their previous techniques of control to gain financial success. The danger in this of course is that the people guiding the journey have no one to guide them, hence the importance of communication and information that give them the necessary awareness, knowledge and skills to be able to utilise this new world effectively.

We are currently experiencing what I would propose is a unique window of opportunity.

Open expression of the deep confusion of our pain and desires is rampant on the Internet and available to millions of people. Either this opportunity can be harnessed to redirect this energy towards greater levels of Conscious Awareness, or the systems that currently control our existence will find a way to control today's technology. This inevitably means they will be controlling the transfer of information, increasing their ability to control us.

Where we stand at present, fear and pain has become a very valuable commodity, and therefore it is spreading through this Information Super-Highway at a rate that far exceeds our ability to decipher and comprehend it.

Most of what we learn today is via these various forms of technology. We have created a situation where a huge proportion of what lives inside our minds, is gathered from information that we have never personally experienced.

Think about the ramifications of that for a moment.

Information is being diluted further and further away from the truth, which therefore makes it easier to control its transfer from mind to mind. This therefore simply empowers the control the Problem-Solving Mind has over us, which enables it to reinforce the structures of the Construct.

PHASE ELEVEN

We are already living in a cyber reality, but now we are creating a cyber version of cyber information!

This could be one of the key reasons behind why psychological pain is becoming so great in today's world, as the ability for Conscious Awareness to attach to the purity of life is becoming further and further removed from its grasp.

The most pure information that we can ever receive is when we are in the midst of nature without any man-made creations to influence our minds. This scenario is obviously becoming harder to find and the societies we are creating are digging deeper into our technological concrete jungles, which are now all linked together via the cyber networks of the Information Super-Highway. In the process of this, even though we have the highest population density that has ever existed on this planet, technology is making our lives more and more isolated from genuine interaction with life and other human beings. The way we communicate with each other is becoming less personal, and therefore making it easier for us to avoid exposing any of our insecurities. Just look at all these new virtual reality worlds that are appearing, where people can develop careers, make money and meet friends, while never leaving the safe confines of their home.

There is however an interesting aspect to this that may eventually work in our favour if we wake up to what is going on. As we are retreating and hiding from face-to-face personal communication, the need for our social cyber guardians is decreasing, and therefore it will be easier to expose and see the true nature and functioning of pain expressed through the Problem-Solving Mind.

So if we smarten up very quickly, there are many aspects of what is happening in the world today that we could quickly turn around and benefit from. However, we don't seem to be fully awake yet as this is not happening. So currently, in our attempts

The Information Super Highway

to appease most of our fears and concerns about life, we are relying on the fact that the information presented to us is founded with truth and integrity - and it is not.

We are being manipulated so quickly and cleverly, that if the Problem-Solving Mind were a person, he or she would be gloating with a smile from ear to ear, as humanity is feeding perfectly into the hands of this super fast transference of distorted information. The further removed we get from the truth, the more our interpretation of life resembles a notion of pain.

> **Technology has become pain's super-fast portal into the human mind for this virus to take over our lives.**

This super-highway of technological information sharing is keeping us united in fear, as fear is the ultimate commodity for the purpose of controlling individuals. And this is whether it is from a government perspective or from the perspective of the big corporations, who have nothing but profit as their ultimate objective. As people are uniting with their pain and the fear that this creates, they are also uniting in their attempts to run away from it as they insatiably seek a solution.

Whilst exploring the Internet, I witness more discussions about the reality of life than I have ever seen before – which makes sense of course. So is this giving us a false perception that things are changing in a direction that is improving humanities chance of survival? I suggest that it is not. Why? Because people are still connecting without understanding the fear that guides human thought. How do I know this? Because people are still linking up with people and ideas they like and avoiding what they don't like – and even when there is some crossover in this regard, I still see the same process of human thought that has always been there. And that is a system of incremental learning where we still live in our concept of future and still justify our ignorance of what needs to change today.

If we understand our minds first, then the nature of how we communicate will change and no longer will we be lost in the future. The future is NOW. The cruelty is happening NOW. The psychological disturbance in the human mind is increasing NOW. Children are abused and used in many countries around the world NOW. Police are being given more power to control us NOW.

This we can all change immediately by changing our awareness and learning how to exist beyond perception and hence share in the truth. Then we need not fear the future, and just start creating it, and then we will not need laws to control us, hence we will be free thinking machines all imbued with integrity and compassion.

Our thinking ability has yet to be even recognised, let alone experienced. I assure you that we could unleash intelligence like we never even imagined if we could just grasp this idea of expansive compassion. If we refuse to collectively stop the cruelty, then that is a sign as to who is running the ship – FEAR!

Waiting at the GoBus stop

The link between government and business (or GoBus) is such that together they are the creator of our fears and the provider of the solutions to them.

Does anyone get a hint of the potential for corruption in this?

Also, governments sell and enforce honesty and integrity, yet the individuals within it display little of these characteristics. They justify their behaviour in the disguise of some greater cause; hence personal responsibility has vanished in some intangible world to which we have lost connection. And on top of all this we are asked to respect and submit to our leaders without questioning their authority! Quite extraordinary when you really stop and think about it. Yet this is the very system of functioning

The Information Super Highway

that the majority of people on this planet are partaking in and contributing to everyday of their lives.

What a masterfully created little system we are experiencing.

Governments feed us with fear, offer to protect us and then control us if we don't do what we are told - quite abhorrent really!

Then in comes the world of business, creating the money that fuels the government machinery. There is certainly no Robin Hood in this story, as the business world does nothing but take advantage of the fear that governments create. The fear they are either knowingly or inadvertently paying the government to create, by supporting these very structures and systems of functioning. One cannot live without the other in this twisted and distorted relationship.

I call this inseparable government and business entity GoBus.

So here we are today united in our fear, problem-solving everything in a desperate attempt to feel good. We believe GoBus is presenting us with the ultimate solution to all our problems, whilst we remain completely unaware that this entity is in fact the devil in disguise.

Technology combined with business acumen, channelled down the Information Super-Highway, which is controlled by governments, is the perfect vehicle for offering the endless lure of happiness. This keeps us chasing something that in reality can never be found as we attempt to escape our pain.

So the system that is continually offering us the false lure of happiness is the same entity that is causing the suffering in the first place. It doesn't matter what position or role we have within this structure, we are ultimately all working for the same team.

PHASE ELEVEN

The human species are all employees of the Construct.

So within this extraordinary structure, where every individual element tends to function as if it is independent from the other, people are, because of their lack of awareness, continuing to feed the pathways that are literally building a super-system of control.

Within this system, technology is being used as the ecstasy pill for adults and youth alike, in an attempt to dull our pain just for long enough to distract us. Meanwhile our fear is being controlled down manipulated pathways. Of course the symbolic ecstasy pill does not take our pain away. It gives us momentary relief and then afterwards leaves us with increased levels of disabling disturbance. Through the clever processes of business indoctrination, we are corralled into a permanent place of wanting more. So we are trying to get on with our life while at the same time feeling stagnant and stationary, as if waiting at the bus stop for the next trip to something good.

Sure enough, the next scheduled GoBus, which symbolises the next alluring and cleverly presented product on the market, comes and picks us up and takes us down another illusionary journey towards everlasting happiness. Although we had momentary relief from our pain, it quickly becomes apparent that it has increased in its intensity when we get dropped off at the next stop – as we think that we got on the wrong bus. Now the pain-driven wanting increases in its concentration, as it also increases the parameters of the thing that is required to satisfy this craving monster that lives within our minds. This also leads us to behave in a more erratic manner, which is dealt with by governments increasing their levels of control. Now that we feel more fear, in comes business like a white knight, to once again solve the problem, offering another product with one extra feature that just might be the very thing we need to be happy!

Let me assure you that business today intensely examines the nature of human thinking via the communication networks that

The Information Super Highway

people are using to unite themselves. It is the younger generation that will have the greatest impact on our future. They have become addicted to the concept of exposing themselves to the world, in some desperate attempt to find recognition, personal fame, acknowledgement, love and friendship – all of the things lacking in their upbringing!

Think of the process I have just described. Now have a look at the rate that new products and services are being created, with all of them offering something bigger and/or better than before. This is because they know what our needs, wants and insecurities are more than ever before. This process is directly correlated to the increasing amount of pain and fear that we are feeling - so it is important to ask yourself if you are any happier for partaking in this process or not. If not, then you are being deceived, manipulated and lied to by the very system that controls you and asks for your trust and financial support. Effectively we are creating the very thing that will eventually destroy us, because we are exposing our fears, wants and desires. This open exposure is being analysed and manipulated behind the scenes at a level that people are generally totally unaware of.

Most people are aware of the underlying discomfort of their existence, but in general they are unaware of the mechanisms that are creating it - particularly in regard to the external systems of their life and the internal mechanisms of their mind that are interpreting and utilising this information.

We have become hopelessly reliant upon the very system that is destroying us and ironically, we created it!

However you want to look at it, if you are able to find a genuine state of strength, wisdom, and happiness in your life, then it is up to you to take charge and make informed and intelligent decisions, not fear-based choices. My advice is to stay away from messages that focus on the outcome of fear and blame while offering no solution or guidance. Also, stay away from any information that feeds your insatiable appetite for quick fix pleasure, whatever the source. Although these may appear to be two totally different forms of information with very different messages, they are in fact one and the same. This is because they are both driven through the processes of the Construct and one cannot live without the other. They are two of the necessary parameters to keep us trapped and undeniably lost within the world of the interactive game in our minds.

Try for one week to disconnect from the Internet, never watch the news and stop reading the newspapers! Be aware of what is guiding your experience of life without being bombarded with all the distorted information, at least until you can honestly say that you are not identifying with your Problem-Solving Mind, until you have the ability to see the truth behind the drama, rather than buying into the fear that it creates.

Media, big business and government's ultimate purpose is to maintain control through the processes of fear and manipulation. This is occurring even though they may individually separate themselves from each other to maintain a place of innocence. But as one cannot live without the other, this is just a convenient justification and an inexcusable process of denial. Within these structures and organisations, the individuals who are making the decisions and enforcing these pathways, do not see the true depth behind the systems they are creating.

If we all stopped and said no, then the insanity could not continue. Otherwise these processes of functioning will march forward until there will be no alternative to live outside of the Construct, as the Construct will become humanity's permanent place of residence.

If you are on the GoBus - get off now!

The last stop is a penal colony that you may never be able to leave.

PHASE TWELVE

What's in it for me?

PHASE TWELVE

We live for our dreams, yet it is our dreams that we can never seem to bring to life, at least not in the way we imagined.

What's in it for me?

Wanting as a survival pathway

As this phase is about wanting I will talk more as 'I' than 'we'.

If I were to look closely at the thoughts and feelings that drive my wanting, I would expose one of the clever illusions that the Problem-Solving Mind creates to keep me trapped in the Construct.

As I am experiencing this global state of insanity, life feels like I have no choice but to succumb to the very systems that are controlling me. When I allow myself to go to this weakened psychological state, I direct my desire to have choice in my personal life.

In the Construct choice represents freedom and it tells me that freedom will be achieved when I get something that I don't already have, hence the concept of wanting.

When I was younger I erroneously believed that my desires had a finite volume, and once full I would remain in a permanent state of happiness. My desires however are infinite and insatiable. Therefore to think that I could find the contentment I so desired, led me into an ever-increasing amount of disillusionment as life progressed. This state of disenchantment was being utilised to control my existence by the very system I was forced from birth to be part of.

> **Wanting is fear of our current situation,
> feeding the notion that life is a
> problem that needs solving.**

People in general do not perceive that their current stage of life is satisfactory because of the pain they experience. They are therefore left to make one simple conclusion. If they attained something that they do not already have, then life will be more peaceful, secure and make more sense – or something of that

197

nature. Hence they see wanting as a necessary mode of thinking in order to gain the control they need to take the pain away and to survive.

Wanting is fear in disguise to mask the processes of pain.

My life is caught in a rather extraordinary process of functioning that most certainly does not serve my purpose, or the purpose of anything else that is connected to my personal life. Yet my fear so convincingly tells me otherwise.

Once I understood where my life was housed I could explore why I was here? Upon my first examination, it appeared that I was in the Construct because everything was serving the best interests of forces like evolution and pain. I can see how people have become heavily attached to and reliant upon the road on which we all currently travel, as they try to maintain some sense of self and some vague semblance of meaning.

My survival mode of functioning is reliant upon the assumption that my learning correctly resembled the structure and functioning of my mind. As each decade progressed on my journey through life, my mind was being left alone without clear guidance or wisdom. The information it was receiving was becoming increasingly distorted and diluted; therefore creating its own version of truth. A truth that I can now see was only a manifestation of fear.

Every thought I have, every opinion and every feeling about every aspect of my life, was actually being created from the process of fear. Therefore, what I was seeing and experiencing was the face of fear, which is Pain's Domain. And the glasses through which I observed the world were filtering out everything other than that pertaining to fear's objectives of control. That is, trying to get what I wanted. This is part of the process that kept me trapped in my cyber reality; as nearly the entirety of my existence was founded on a notion of what happiness is.

What's in it for me?

As the levels of fear in my life increased, my belief in the process of wanting also increased, so I therefore mistakenly attached ever-increasing levels of hope to wanting as a solution. This continued to feed the fear and so on it goes.

> **By becoming addicted to wanting we have become addicted to fear, which means that our whole existence is an addiction of some kind.**

I asked myself if I did not use fear as a guide in my life then how would I know what to do? Or at the very least how would I know what I want and how to get it?

Of course, this is presuming that getting what I wanted would take away the fear. But of course it didn't, because I was chasing a concept that exists in a certain mindset - a never-ending one. The end result was that the Problem-Solving Mind was trying to gain full control over my existence, whereby it was becoming nothing but a cyber reality.

My cyber reality is a perceptual reality - it is not truth and yet somehow it tries to convince me that my individual reality is the truth and that other people's realities are not. I resisted the desire to fight for what I believed, as ultimately this was just about getting what I wanted.

My beliefs were creating a false sense of security. They mislead me into thinking that they were a solid structure that I could rely upon to determine the nature of what I wanted. However, every belief that I created became another bar in the prison of my mind. A prison that just kept me further and further detached from reality and falling deeper into the black hole of wanting.

> **So wanting without high levels of awareness is in fact insanity!**

Walking a tight rope

When the Construct guided my existence, my life was in a process of trying to get what I wanted and I felt the need to be right. When I convinced myself that I was right, I was solidifying my beliefs to create the illusion of strength.

As I continued down this controlling and insatiable pathway, I remained stuck on a tight rope which represented my wanting - one small and insignificant aspect of my journey. And my wanting is a representative of fear and my fear is controlling what I think life is.

Even though I feel the danger of falling off this tight rope at any moment, in this state I feel that I must stick to its tiny and narrow parameters, as I am effectively blind beyond it. Wanting puts me into a thinking pattern that is very single-minded and obsessive, and therefore excludes anything that does not appear to be able to help me attain my desires.

The reason this tight rope is so addictive is because it leads me to feel that if I fall off this dangerously narrow pathway that I will conceptually die. That is because I cannot see what lies beneath me. However, I realised that what lay beneath me was everything outside of my wanting - the completeness of life.

So there are three identifiable issues here that were trying to stop me from taking a leap of faith:

Firstly, my vision had become so narrow and focused on moving straight ahead that I could not actually see the entirety of what is. Secondly, even if I were to look down to respond to a message from life that is beyond these parameters, I would not understand nor recognise this realm, and therefore not trust it. This leaves only one option, to hold on tightly to what I already know. Thirdly, I was still buying into the notion that I was at the mercy of what I could see, rather than realising that I am the creator of all that I experience, and wanting disguises this reality.

What's in it for me?

So inevitably I end up stuck in a place of wanting, which has been created from my beliefs, in the false notion that happiness always lies ahead from where I currently stand. This leaves a permanent gap between where I am and where I want to be; hence my Problem-Solving Mind is forever trying to work out how to solve this dilemma.

Of course this gap is not real, as I am chasing the notion of what I think will make me happy, based on what I have learnt or dreamt of in the past.

> **As I travel along my tight rope of fear-based wanting, the concept of happiness is pushed forward as I move forward.**

Even if I do get to a destination that somewhat resembles my desires, I will quickly notice that any sensation of happiness is short lived. Therefore, I would redirect my attention once again to a life ahead of me. The reason for this is because the Problem-Solving Mind gets a taste of what it thinks it wants and then instantly directs this sensation into the future. It then tries to problem-solve how to create a situation where it can maintain this feeling permanently.

This feeling is not genuine happiness, but only cyber happiness, so therefore it can never be maintained. The Problem-Solving Mind directs everything experienced in the Construct - and this ensures that I must be in a permanent state of discomposure (the sensation I feel when I am emotionally repressed). This repression is created from not allowing myself to *be* the experience while trying to chase aspects of it.

Like pieces of the puzzle

When my Construct is guiding my existence I am constantly juggling life and trying to change and rearrange the pieces of the puzzle in my cyber reality. I feel frantic as I try to create a picture that matches my notion of self. A notion of how I want life to be, in order to satisfy my beliefs, needs and insatiable greed.

Even when I am asleep my brain gives me no rest, as I desperately try to work out the answers to getting what I want in my subconscious dream state. The Problem-Solving Mind is never inactive whether I know it or not, and this is why it is such a powerful mechanism. If I am not living in a state of complete awareness, the Problem-Solving Mind has great control over me whilst I am effectively unconscious. It uses dreams to help create the necessary illusions to keep me either in a state of fear, or in a state of desiring things that do not exist - in reality, both are one and the same thing. But if I did not know this, I would jump back and forth from one to the other, thinking that somehow this is creating motion in my life. The puzzle now seems even more complicated with more pieces to put in place.

So what is my reward on this pathway?

The answer is that I am rewarded with a brief moment of sanity - a moment where there seems to be no problems that need solving, where I can actually indulge in the satisfaction of success.

Think about any moment in your life when you felt great, or take note next time when you do - and see whether you perceive anything whatsoever to be a problem that needs solving.

As mentioned above, this moment is quite brief (relatively speaking) and the pleasure I receive potentially drives me back into the insanity in the belief that the next moment will be one that I can hold onto, thereby maintaining my sanity and happiness forever.

Wanting is dangerous

If I am in a state of wanting and I do not get what I want I will potentially fall apart very quickly, depending of course on the intensity of the wanting.

What's in it for me?

These two factors work in direct correlation with each other:

The greater the level of wanting, the greater the level of pain when I don't get what I want.

However the more I want, the more satisfaction I feel when I do get what I want. Unfortunately, this can convince me that wanting is an acceptable and favourable process of thinking, and that the solution is to get clearer and more focused about what I want and how to get there. But even high levels of pleasure will not be sustainable. My mind will become even more fearful of losing this experience, and then it will very quickly draw its attention onto what else it needs to maintain this feeling. It will either want more from the thing that it has attained, hence the desire to control, or it will look beyond this thing and start wanting something else.

Wanting is all about the need to receive.

It negates the process of giving.

And we cannot truly receive until we learn to give.

True giving means learning to be fully cognisant of the needs of others – otherwise, what are you giving? The act of giving means being Consciously Aware. It means I am able to receive from life, to feel whole as I no longer get lost in wanting! I am living in a mode of functioning that constantly believes happiness lies in the future. The Problem-Solving Mind can never be satisfied when it gets what it wants; otherwise its purpose would be void. This mode of thinking is not necessarily wrong. It is just very dangerous when it is only guided by fear, and when there is no wisdom and Conscious Awareness attached to the process.

Playing it safe

As life progressed I discovered that getting what I want created high levels of stress. This could, if I was not aware of these factors in my reality, lead me towards a life of playing it safe, keeping my wanting within secure and tangible parameters.

> However, wanting is wanting, irrespective of how safe the target is that you are aiming at.
>
> Or, on the other side of the coin, how great a target I am aiming at – like changing the direction of human thought for example.

The point I am really trying to illustrate is that it doesn't matter what I want, one way or another I will constantly keep myself trapped in the world of pain and fear – trapped in a maze with no exit.

> Nothing is mine to *get* in the first place as wanting ties in with the notion of control and ownership.

The law of diminishing returns

When I was young, I was full of dreams, hope and desires. I believed in them so strongly that the gap between where I was and where I would like to be did not bother me. I actually thought that because I wanted something I would get it. I believed these things existed because I saw other people with them. At one point I had the desire to be a movie star because the movie stars' lives seemed full of reward and recognition. I had a desire to be rich and successful because rich and successful people appeared to be happy. I imagined it this way because I wanted what they had and I believed if I had it, everything would be okay.

However, as the journey of life continued, these dreams got further and further away because they were never real in the first place. I realised I could either keep chasing dreams and become more disillusioned, or wake up and face the truth of my existence without editing what I see for my own convenience.

This is the law of diminishing returns.

The longer I forged on into the world of wanting, the less I felt life was giving back. It doesn't matter what I get or what I achieve, it feels like it is worthless owing to the increasing levels of pain and dissatisfaction that arise. Right from the beginning in my childhood, I was actually building two mental pathways of thinking at the same time. One is the process of expanding my vision of what life could be around my dreams, the other is the fear and concern of how to get it and that I might not get it at all. These two pathways of thought may start at the same point but from that moment on they are heading off on divergent tracks.

It became very apparent to me that I had inadvertently attached two ways of thinking to the one concept and each of these ways continued to grow further apart. Even though I kept modifying and changing the notion of what it is I thought I wanted, the doubt and fear of never being happy kept blazing its own trail in a very different direction.

Eventually I became extremely disillusioned, because the gap between where I perceived myself to be and where I perceived I would like to be felt massive. The enormity of this gap got so great that I eventually saw my dreams as something negative that causes high levels of pain.

However, I discovered that there was no need to give up on my dreams. I realised the importance of becoming Consciously Aware, and now my dreams inspire me as they grow out of an unedited place! Now my dreams grow from the essence of me, hence they feel more purposeful, and I continually inject more awareness into them to dissolve the fear that can halt their manifestation into reality. Awareness embodies integrity whilst wanting embodies corruption. To get what I want, I will always have to trade my integrity and I am not prepared to do this once I am aware wanting is driving my existence. If I traded my integrity for a perceptual gain I would destroy any chance of waking up to a state of Conscious Awareness. The illusion created by the Construct therefore becomes harder and harder to see through, as this process of thought reinforces the cage in which one resides.

PHASE THIRTEEN

I need to be more!

PHASE THIRTEEN

Wanting to be something

So what does all of this wanting really mean?

Ultimately it is the Problem-Solving Mind trying to create some form of identity and meaning in its existence. This is why it is always so obsessed in trying to be something other than what it currently is.

To delve deeper into this topic I will share a story with you.

One night I was out to dinner with a group of people and somebody paid particular attention to my area of interest, that being human behaviour. She was intelligent, attractive and very well presented, and she asked me to give my opinion on what I thought of her. Rather than doing that, I simply asked her to tell me about herself. Her response was to explain that the most important thing in her life was to learn how to just be; in fact she went on to express that it was her chosen mission in life. So I asked her that if she actually *wanted* to learn to be, did this mean she was currently trying to be something other than herself? She quite defensively asserted that she was not pretentious, and that she is herself and does not present a fake front to the world - "I am only ever me," she said.

This was an interesting response for someone who wants to learn to just be!

I did not wish to confront her unnecessarily so I asked if she would like me to continue the discussion, to which she agreed. I began by challenging her thinking and asked her to explain, by the very nature of her *wanting* to learn to be, what was she now? Was she pursuing something that she currently didn't perceive herself to be, a place or notion that she felt she must journey to, to be happy or content?

She paused in silence for a few minutes and then looked at me with a deep sense of awareness.

She smiled and said, "You are right, I have been trying to be something. I have never thought about it like this before. How could I already be *being* myself, if my life mission has become to learn to just be?" She again sat silently with a sense of knowing and calm, and although she had not experienced this state of being before, she found it easy to accept. For a moment her Conscious Awareness was alive!

This conversation, as simple as it is, has a lot of truth embodied in it, so let's explore further.

To be or not to be - is not a fictional question!

I discovered early on in my life that by the very nature of me trying to be something meant I was not being me.

Based on what you have learnt so far, ask yourself the following questions and take a moment to see what answers you come up with. What does trying to be something really mean? Why would you try to be something for that matter? How would you know if you were trying to be something or just being you? Does this propose that we are insane for behaving in such a manner?

> Trying to be something was nothing more
> than a survival pathway leading my life.

Trying to be something is the foundation of what wanting is all about. As previously mentioned, it is the Problem-Solving Mind's belief that true happiness, security and love, live in a place somewhere other than where I currently am. Of course, it thinks this, because the Construct denies these qualities of life to be anything other than a notion. They are desires that can only be experienced for brief moments, before the mind quickly moves on to the next problem to solve.

PHASE THIRTEEN

Let's explore the question that I asked the young lady at the dinner party:

> **'If you want to learn to *be* then does that mean you are currently trying to be something other than you?'**

By the very nature of this question, if you want to learn to just be, then you are pursuing something that you currently are not; otherwise you would already be it.

This philosophy, as simple as it is, opened up a very important topic in my mind which lead to a realm of understanding that transformed my life - from searching for the insatiable questions of being, to the truth of Isness.

Isness is not being - Isness just is.

Isness is life unedited.

Isness and the understanding of it was a portal to a place in the mind where my experience could be explored without fear and my creativity could be unleashed. There is an Isness to who I am, a truth, a reality that defies any perception or notion of my life. In this mode of functioning, I give myself to life without editing. Hence everything that comes back makes sense and therefore I remove myself from the process of wanting, which removes me from the processes of fear.

I acknowledge that I exist in a state that is primarily obsessed with maintaining its existing belief structure, hence the physical self. This perceptual reality is very limiting, as its whole basis for creating an existence is dictated by the need to protect the physical self, where its guide is fear.

The concept of who I think I am is a permanently insecure and ever changing reality that will create great stress as I try and keep it under control. This becomes painful because I am trying to be the parts of the experience that I think I want, rather than being the whole experience.

If you are trying to work out whom and what you are, then it is good evidence that you are living in your Construct. Or at the very least your Construct is dominating your thinking and your experience of being you. If you stay addicted to your cyber reality then you will be permanently trying to create and maintain some idea of self that satisfies your insecurity. And by the very nature of what insecurity is, it can never be satisfied – and why satisfy it anyway?

> Wanting is derived from insecurity.
>
> Without insecurity I would not want.

Time is an illusion

The illusion that time is a tangible reality that I can control was created by my observations that the physical realm changes around me.

It is only in my mind that I actually have a past and a future. This leads me to feel that I am at the mercy of the physical world and therefore I must try to create a 'me' that fits in with what we see. I witnessed other people so desperately attaching themselves to a group that has a type of behaviour and a certain look. They were literally living as a programmed entity without any true individuality within their expression of self. I can see this when I observe many young people, who erroneously believe they are expressing their individuality by following a group that is either separate to, or at odds with the mainstream flow of society. Either way, it is still just a group and they are still just following a notion of self in an attempt to try and create an identity.

Instead of looking at the physical realm as something I must control and hence master, I look at it as something that just is what it is. Something I am not going to control, but instead let the Isness of my existence merge into one with it, because I am it whether I know it or not!

And to do this I need to relinquish my obsession with time.

If I don't I will always feel like I am running out of time. I would become more focussed on getting as much as I can from the world before I run out of time. I decided, as best I could, to forget time and just trust in the journey of understanding my existence. For without that what I am really doing rushing around filling up time?

In my cyber reality I am everything that I see, everything that I touch, everything that I feel and everything that I think, smell and taste. My Problem-Solving Mind is in effect the creator of the world that I witness. However, this is a world of artificial intelligence. It exists, but it is not life or me that I am experiencing, just a cyber version of it. Hence the insatiable journey of trying to find oneself – one can't find what does not exist. I can create an endless list of versions of what I think I am, however one day it will all get so confusing that the temptation will be to give up.

The real me exists in the Isness, a place of no time and no wanting.

By wanting 'to be' I create a vision of a place, I then create a vision of myself within this place, and I therefore try to create a life that will bring this vision to a state of reality. A place that I think exists somewhere in my perceptual continuum of time. My mind tries to convince me that everything I want will exist in a place where I can finally relax and be happy. The notion of this place and me within it is of course all one and the same. In the perceptual realm I am whatever I imagine, so if I imagine beauty I feel beauty. Hence imaging a place and me in it is all me within

I need to be more!

that concept, and this can be very confusing to a mind that is trying to work out what it is.

Peace for me came from letting go of the concept of wanting to be something, in fact from letting go of wanting full stop.

This might be a strange thought at first, however, consider that we are letting notions, which are created from our belief structure, guide and lead us in an attempt to interact with life itself. What we are actually experiencing is not life, but just an edited interpretation of it.

I will never continue to experience Isness as long as I stay trapped in a world of functioning that is focussed on its fear of death, and the obsession with time that grows out of this.

Do we want to live our lives in a world of 'should be', or 'could be', or in a world of 'Isness'?

Just because 'Isness' is not what we want it to be, does not change what it is!

Some could perceive the following as 'bad news', but for me it is the truth nevertheless. Isness is simply the way things are, but this does not mean that I will necessarily feel good. For example, if suffering surrounded me then I feel that suffering. The difference is that it would not be attached to my life story; therefore I would be able to handle whatever it was that I was experiencing and give myself to the situation accordingly. From here my life has a sense of purpose without looking for purpose, as I have no denial. I give the best I can to all that I experience without self-absorbed greed.

So imagine if we could all collectively stop wanting for just a brief moment...

And feel the truth of all that is happening on this planet.

If we could feel the pain and suffering of all that we destroy in the attainment of our desires . . .

> Our minds would drown in tears of sorrow and remorse. And in the death of our denial, we would be reborn.

We would now be AWARE!

Once aware we could no longer get lost in wanting, as we would be giving of ourselves through a place of compassion. If this were possible for us all to feel the truth, then the journey of self-absorbed misery would come to an end.

> Humanity would finally be free!

And if this experience did not wake us up then I don't think an ongoing journey of advanced consciousness is awaiting humanity.

Watch yourself for one whole day. Take with you a pen and paper and count how many times you get agitated, frustrated, angry or annoyed. Notice that these emotions only occur when you don't get what you want. The traffic is busier than you wanted it to be. Somebody spoke to you in a way that you didn't like. Your dinner in the restaurant was not presented the way you wanted it to be.

Try to see the illness in our wanting, the insanity of buying into the notion that the world could somehow accommodate what we want, and what we perceive to be right or wrong. It would appear that everybody is trapped in the Construct so nobody is genuinely considerate to the needs of others unless it pertains to their own notion of survival.

When I do submit to what others want from me, it is because I see some gain in it, even if that gain is to keep myself safe. So in this particular situation, I would like to point out that this is not 'giving' in the pure sense of the word. It is giving for the process of manipulation to get what I want. This process of functioning just keeps recycling itself from one situation to another.

My brain tries to continually function this way to make sense of life. For if the Problem-Solving Mind was to stop and look at itself for too long, it would panic in the reality of seeing its own insanity and become disillusioned by its own insatiable desires – never coming to terms with the fact that it is not actually a human being as such, rather just a notion of one!

When wanting becomes obsessive

Do you find in your life that you must keep constantly active to maintain some sense of sanity? Do you have the courage to stop long enough to see the insanity of your own behaviour?

Think about people you have met that have to be constantly busy and achieving. Do you think these people are totally lost in the world of wanting; desperately trying to attain that next brief moment of satisfaction one feels when they are successful?

If we can see the truth of our functioning, we might find the key to being released from the prison of our own making. The prison we actually think is the world. The prison we think represents the limitations of reality. When in reality it is the limitations of our own perception.

I can feel that the functioning of the Problem-Solving Mind is programmed into the reality of my DNA structure. This programming appears to be in everybody. How this programming manifests within each individual person and what we think we want out of life, is dependent upon the nature of our learning and our genetic personality. The Insanity of Humanity is the fact that we do not seem to be able to see that we are at the mercy of complex programs.

> We as a species have become blind and in the darkness we have become scared.

To feel the process of giving without wanting is to feel life outside of the Problem-Solving Mind. It is to feel life to the absolute depths of our emotional realm within the purity of what is. Isness is what I present. For in this realm of life our connections do not need to be controlled. Control is only necessary when we live in the house of fear, the fear of not getting what we want!

Dream chasers

Think about our learning as children.

What do we look forward to more than anything else? A lot of children in a lot of different countries look forward to Christmas Day! Hence they are looking forward to something that does not actually exist in the way it has been sold to them. Do you think this is healthy?

This topic certainly creates interesting debates in discussion groups or when I have presented it at various talks. The most common response is quite a heated one, because people's Problem-Solving Minds quickly step in to protect and defend the part of its Construct that is being challenged and threatened. Why? Because Christmas Day is a heavily reinforced aspect of our learning, and therefore as far as the Construct is concerned, part of whom we identify as being us.

Of course I am not debating whether we should, or should not keep Christmas Day as a time of celebration. However, what I would like you to consider is that we are teaching our children to live for the future. We teach them to believe in something that is not real. We teach them to become obsessed about material possessions. We teach them that happiness lies somewhere outside their own self. And to top it all off, we wait until they are old enough, shatter their dreams and tell them that the whole thing was a lie right from the beginning!

I need to be more!

I am simply using this as an example for how we tend to approach all of life and where this learning comes from in our childhood. Because we learned to function this way as children, we impose the same learning on our children, thus sending them on the insatiable pathway of wanting.

Many of the false notions and dreams that I chased in regard to how I would like to look, the person I would like to be, the partner I would like to find and the general way that I would like to live, came from fantasy stories.

> **We live in a world becoming increasingly obsessed with fantasy because we are experiencing so little of reality.**

These two forces work in direct correlation with each other. As we are creating societies where technology is removing us further away from nature and intimate personal relationships, our desire for fantasy increases as a replacement. This can be seen in the increasing popularity of 3D movies, computer games, pornography, and Internet sites like Facebook and virtual reality worlds.

The mother-ship of anxiety

To live in a wanting mode is to live at the mercy of the future, and at the mercy of time. My concern that I will not get what I want in the future, is one of the key constants for the creation of any anxiety I experience.

Anxiety is always linked to the future.

So if we want to live a life without anxiety, then stop wanting!

In addition, if we get to a point where we must face the realisation that we will never get what we want, anxiety can quickly turn into depression.

PHASE THIRTEEN

To surmise

When we are 'wanting' we are chasing a notion and a feeling. The 'thing' we are chasing is in fact irrelevant. This will vary depending on our beliefs and learning.

We have all sorts of things that we want to do with our lives, all sorts of dreams and visions. We all dream of having a certain kind of partner or doing a certain type of job or living in a certain country. The only things stopping us from attaining our visions in a tangible sense are our fear-based programs that have created the life we are currently in, the one we are unhappy with. Everything we create through a process of fear will ultimately leave us feeling unhappy. When we get trapped in these programs of functioning our life never seems to really improve, and deep down in our subconscious we judge this by how we feel; not by what we own, or how much we earn, or how physically beautiful our partner is. Because if that is what our programs wanted us to have, or were constructed to allow us to have, we would have them and feel great about it. There would be no need for wanting at all, as we would be getting so much from what is. So if everything we have is not making us feel good, then fear-based programs, rather than the truth of our existence, created these things.

Initially when people try to embrace the idea of not wanting, their perceptual notion of time diminishes. Their dreams seem further and further away. It is like being stranded on an island, feeling helpless and trapped, watching a ship fade slowly into the distance as it heads out to sea. On that ship are all of their hopes, dreams, wants and desires. That ship represents the person they thought they could be and needed to be, to be happy. It eventually feels so intangible and out of their reach that they just give up on themselves and on life, and that means they are now nothing but their Problem-Solving Mind trapped in the world of wanting. However, if they sit and watch this ship disappearing into the distance, without seeing it as a problem, they will eventually feel the freedom of realising that they don't need it and all that it encompasses.

So stop wanting, as wanting implies choice.

To make a choice implies that life happens in bits and pieces, in broken down segments of time. As life is a constant thing that always exists, it cannot be broken down into choices. There is effectively an infinite amount of factors permanently influencing the reality of everything all of the time.

Life just is. Life is not a choice.

Now that we have explored the idea of Isness as opposed to wanting, it is very important to note that once you see life through an unedited reality, you do not have to think this means acceptance. For example, the current processes of life and human thought are completely unacceptable to me; hence my inspiration to explore other possibilities of existence. So stay open about how you will feel when you stop editing life's information – you will just know!

PHASE FOURTEEN

Nature's intention

PHASE FOURTEEN

In vain desperation we try to reconfigure our existing knowledge on human functioning, in an attempt to find the peace that we so frantically seek in our minds.

So what was nature's intention?

Nature, creation, evolution, God or some form of alien intelligence formed the world that you and I are living in now. Whatever your beliefs are in regard to this topic, or wherever the truth lies in all of this is to some degree irrelevant. Because whatever the cause, one thing we can be sure of, we are experiencing something!

It is a matter of understanding what that 'something' is.

In so many ways this world is an amazing place to exist in. Yet, despite the obvious beauty, suffering and death are necessary for life to continue. Everything is eating another living creature to survive.

> **It doesn't matter how you look at it, lots of things must die in order for something to live.**

Is this wrong? Or is it just the way it is?

There is only one species on this planet that has the necessary levels of Conscious Awareness to know what they are eating and whether suffering is attached to that process - and that is human beings. But we don't use that awareness, as we continue to partake in the consumption of life for the continuance of our own. And the amount of animals that humans kill every year numbers in the billions.

I don't think there would be too much argument in regard to the fact that this process was necessary for us to survive in more primitive times. But was it nature's intention that we should continue along this course and accept the suffering that is created in the process of our own survival?

Whether it was nature's intention or not does not really matter, as we have the ability to do otherwise, and this fact in itself could indicate that the answer to the question is yes. If we opened up our minds, we would not have to knowingly kill any other creature in order to live out our existence. Irrespective of this, we justify that the current mode of functioning of our behaviour is just a way of life. Just the way it is!

Well yes, it is this way at present. But why would we fight to protect and defend a way of life that is primitive, cruel and basic from an awareness perspective? And this is not Isness; this is denial and manipulation of information to create a pathway of thought and corresponding action to suit that one particular individual.

Sitting in and seeing the Isness of life does not mean that you have to accept it or surrender to it. If it feels unhealthy, then it does. That too is Isness. In fact resistance when channelled through awareness is exactly what is required to find new ways to exist - to evolve!

So why do we still justify our contribution to the cruelty, especially when we consider that the same process can turn back on us at any moment? Suddenly we are no longer the predator and we become the prey. It certainly doesn't feel good when we are on the less desirable side of the coin. In fact, most of us would scream out in indignant fear, begging for help and for someone to save us.

Compassion when turned on and off to suit our own needs is not compassion at all, just convenient processes of thinking. For example, if we're only compassionate to human suffering then we are not actually being compassionate. We, by being human, fear the notion of experiencing the same type of pain that leads us to want to help others. This is how the Construct guides our thinking whether we are aware of it or not.

The essence behind all I have proposed here and the questions that I have asked, underlies the reasoning behind everything that we are doing that is destroying our planet, our home.

It is not just *our* home; it is the home of every single living entity that exists on this planet – and some of those entities are sentient beings just like us. Although the majority of them do not have the power to speak up for their lives to be treated with respect, does not excuse our abuse of power to abuse their emotional world. We can continue to justify the manner in which we exercise our domination over other living things, but ultimately it will not just lead to the demise of their lives, but also of our own. Let me reiterate something important to consider and ask yourself where you sit relative to this statement:

The true test of humanity's current level of awareness is exposed in the way we treat those things that we are not forced to treat with compassion or kindness...

Whether that be people, animals or our planet. Do you consider the life and suffering of an animal before you eat it? Do you stop to help the wild animal that has been hit by a car? Most people don't and if they do they rarely act on this awareness. Why? Because getting what they want is more important than the integrity of how they acquire it. They have a destination of happiness to find, so they can't let too much else get in the way. It is in our treatment of animals that the corruption in our thinking is most readily exposed, hence why I use it as an example to illustrate my point.

Some people debate with me that we are the superior species, proclaiming that they have the right to do whatever they want. I wonder if these people would graciously give this justification in behaviour to an advanced alien species should they make it to Earth, as they lock us inside little cages while preparing us for their dinner! They may even find it useful to keep us alive while draining various substances from our organs - doesn't sound so bad does it? I mean it can't be 'bad' can it? Because people on the whole accept and contribute to such things every day of their lives. What they don't know, is that to partake in such behaviour is actually feeding the illusion that is destroying their lives and all of humanity – we really are the sacrificial lamb, and while lost in our ignorance and pride, we gloat and indulge in our power and all that this can provide for us.

So . . . what is going on inside your mind right now? Awareness – or indifference?

I have helped many individuals on their journey into awareness, and the majority have stopped eating animals without me ever mentioning this topic. They found this truth by becoming aware. The process of unleashing their compassion beyond their Construct allowed them to feel equally for all living creatures. Now there is no longer a choice as to whether or not they can turn a blind eye to the suffering of others - it just is. They now act on this awareness rather than justifying and defending their existing thoughts.

However, if you are still confused about what I am saying, give yourself a break, for it is not you that is consuming life, it is pain via the pathways of your Problem-Solving Mind.

I too was brought up eating other living beings and it took me many years to wake up to the insanity of what I was partaking in and how divergent this was from me growing into a mature and caring man.

Pain when misunderstood allows for the justification of just about anything in the right circumstances. So the Problem-Solving Mind is simply being true to nature's intention as we speak. However, we as living entities that are alive with Conscious Energy have the ability to redirect this, not just for our own good, but also for the cause of life itself.

Nature's weapon

Nature certainly created the ultimate piece of thinking machinery to keep us trapped in the existing processes of evolution. However, it also created the unbelievable possibility for us to break free of this. But first we need to clearly understand the nature of these mechanisms that are disallowing our freedom.

The Construct is necessary for the functioning of the Problem-Solving Mind, which is developed for the behaviour of a child, or for that of a relatively primitive creature; a being that does not have the ability to interact with life via the peaceful pathways of wisdom and awareness.

As the Problem-Solving Mind creates beliefs, which are founded in fear, it will protect and defend them when challenged. It is not necessary that we bring our beliefs with us as we journey into our adult lives, but this is exactly what we are doing. Therefore, they become somewhat rigid, corrupt, and distorted as we continue to try and enforce them on the world as if they are the truth. Of course this leaves us with nothing but continuing frustration and disturbance.

I know only too well from my own life how difficult it is to leave our beliefs behind, particularly in light of the fact that I have not met anyone else doing the same thing. I am not saying that there are not people doing this but I have not met them. So doing this alone whilst others are still fighting for their beliefs is challenging, hence the importance for the human race to find a common place of understanding. But it starts with one person, and then two, and on it goes!

Imagine a wolf cub

Let's look at the development of a Construct within the functioning of an intelligent and emotionally driven creature on this planet, other than human.

Most young creatures grow up relying on their parents to teach them the ways of life. Through a process of learning they develop skills to take advantage of their genetic realities. Their learning is coming from many years of carefully developed survival techniques that have worked from generation to generation. All of this learning makes total sense within the mind of the creature absorbing it.

Through the process of evolution and survival of the fittest, a wolf exists harmoniously in its environment. The learning that has transferred from generation to generation is totally appropriate to the genetic reality of this creature and to the environment in which it exists. Via all of this appropriate and healthy learning from its parents, the cub develops into a full-grown wolf. It now fulfils its purpose and role within the hierarchy of its social group. It has developed a Construct that guides its journey in a healthy and functional manner and there is no need to look past this. Because of the limited thinking capabilities of the mind within this Construct, the destruction to life and other living things is limited to that which is only pertaining to the creature's immediate survival. A wolf's mind is programmed to work by association - a very basic system for dealing with life that creates a lot of disorder and problems, especially when applied to human beings living in a more complicated world.

We absorb large amounts of disturbing information that do not make sense within the confines of our own genetic makeup. As we progress through life, continuing to learn by association, we end up fearing more and more things giving rise to many psychological conditions such as anxiety, depression and phobias. That is, irrational fear where there is no real and present danger - but as far as the mind is concerned the danger is real. It cannot discern the difference between perception and reality and it is programmed to believe what its learning tells it.

The more inappropriate our learning, the more irrational is the nature of our fear and our corresponding behaviour. When we cannot emotionally handle our fears we try to control what we think is causing this pain.

The dart theory

Because we are the masters of problem-solving, we have been able to adapt to extreme environmental changes and as a consequence the journey of our species continues. This means our mind, unlike a wolf's, is capable of taking us into situations that have very little to do with whether or not our genetic makeup is cohesive with the environment in which we are entering.

Consider our human ancestors as they began to spread across the planet over many thousands of years. In this time they created an extremely interesting genetic diversity that is not necessarily conducive to our lives making any sense.

The further we remove ourselves from an environment that matches our genetic makeup, the more powerfully the Problem-Solving Mind steps in to take over our lives. It now must build its own environment to suit its own functioning. Now more than ever on this planet our physical capabilities have little to do with whether we survive or not. Also, with the advent of the rapid technological advances witnessed in the last century, we have once again further removed ourselves from our physical being offering us clues as to the purpose of our existence. Yet because of the functioning of the Problem-Solving Mind, we still behave as if our physical existence is who and what we are. In fact we are more obsessed with it now than ever before!

The result of this is that we are living in a world in which our genetic makeup does not match our physical environment. Our learning has almost nothing to do with our innate purpose, let alone where our spirit fits into all of this.

> **Where we were born has as much meaning and substance as if our lives started as a dart being thrown randomly at the spinning world.**

From wherever this dart should land, we are effectively on our own, struggling to work out the nature of our existence and how to survive. Even worse, we have to do this with learning that is dysfunctional and inappropriate, while at the same time being driven by forces beyond our control and understanding. In fact, given that our primary learning influence comes from our parents and given that they are functioning through a world of distorted fear, it is not surprising why everybody is lost and confused.

The reality of this dynamic is perfect for the Problem-Solving Mind and the Construct to maintain control over our very existence.

It is time that we discover a more effective and peaceful way to function, because we are still relying on the same system of learning and development that was necessary for us to exist in more primitive times. It is simply not appropriate in the world we live in today, and this is forcing us to have to look beyond the parameters of our lives.

I encourage all of humanity to cease enforcing the primitive pathways along which we are all currently walking. Initially this can be done by relinquishing the control that the Problem-Solving Mind has over us. This may sound hypocritical, but for the Problem-Solving Mind to continue its reign over our lives, it is necessary for us to fight and struggle with the reality of our own minds. That is what we are all doing as we bury ourselves deep within our own psychological nightmares.

Let's clarify what I have just proposed. The Problem-Solving Mind and its ability to conquer its external environment is almost too smart for its own good. In the process of its insatiable desire to satisfy its needs and its determination to survive, it has driven us into environments and into social structures which have very little to do with the nature of our being. It is our environment that determines our belief structures, whether they are appropriate to us or not.

Even though it may appear that the Problem-Solving Mind is experiencing great levels of pain, it is certainly managing to fulfil its apparent destiny of control. One could easily conclude that the external dynamics of our lives seem to have no rhyme or reason, other than to lure us towards a state of happiness that will always remain beyond our reach. We are trying to find something that does not exist by using the part of the brain that got us into this situation in the first place!

However, it does not matter what the Problem-Solving Mind is trying to get, it will never be satisfied because the nature of its functioning denies this possibility. In fact, it is structured such that if life were to resemble something in the order of what would make us content, the Problem-Solving Mind would create drama in order to create problems to give itself a sense of purpose. When it has a sense of purpose it can almost start to believe that it is actually real - even though it cannot work out how to get close to its vision of where it thinks happiness lives.

To what degree the Problem-Solving Mind knows what it's doing is debatable. Although it is the creator of our experiential reality, it is quite possibly just a tool being used by other forces in the same manner that it uses to control us.

Either the Problem-Solving Mind is unable to truly absorb the entirety of life's information, hence leaving it no option but to create a virtual reality, or it knows exactly what it's doing, absorbs and embraces every aspect of life as it experiences it, and then selectively provides us with the necessary information to keep us trapped.

Please note as you explore this book regarding the functioning of the Problem-Solving Mind; always keep the possibilities of what is actually going on very open and flexible. I suggest this because we are all living in a world of illusion, and it would therefore be wise to always keep our minds open as to what is real and what is not.

Life in a room

Imagine what would happen if a person were locked in a room

PHASE FOURTEEN

from the time they were born, with their basic survival needs taken care of. Until the age of 20 they have no control over what learning takes place in that room. I am sure it would be quite easy to accept that the structure of that person's thinking and their behavioural characteristics would be heavily influenced by the stimuli they were subjected to.

For example; if all he or she saw were videos of violence and destruction, then one would presume this person would develop a multitude of irrational fears, and this would be reflected in the development of their Construct. Let alone the effects of being locked in a room for 20 years. They would have no point of comparison so this would become their reality.

Once they were released into the 'real world', their sense of reality would be extremely distorted and many degrees of separation from the truth. Primarily their mind would be in a complete state of illusion, and therefore their emotional responses would not be effectively corresponding to what was actually happening around them. The end-result of this would be that the person would become incredibly stressed, anxious, depressed and confused.

The sad reality, although our learning is rarely this extreme, is that most people's lives are a version of what I have just described. Think of the room as a representation of our learning. This learning creates the box that we are all trapped in and it is the visual representation of the psychological cage that controls our lives.

Do you think because you didn't grow up in one room that your life has more freedom?

Unless you were taught, or figured it out yourself, that you are not your Construct, then the size of the room is irrelevant. You can't leave planet Earth, not yet anyway, so think of this as the box. Of course it has nothing to do with where you grew up, whether it is in a room or roaming the whole planet. It is your learning (and the beliefs they create) that become the box in which you exist - the restrictive parameters of your existence.

We are simply interpreters of what our senses receive and from this information we attempt to form a sense of reality relevant to our internal emotional forces. The less appropriate our learning, and the more detached our genetics are from our environment, the more we will feel disturbed and hence live in a more distorted illusionary state.

> Irrespective of the nature of the learning, it is still an illusion.

This really is the key point all of us need to absorb. This is because we seem to think that one type of learning is better than another, or that one person's life is more fortunate - but it isn't. It is all the same thing in a different disguise. Otherwise we will keep fighting to enforce what we feel as we believe it to be the truth, and never understand why our actions don't lead to positive outcomes.

If your life feels terribly wrong, then more than likely you have got to the point where you can no longer believe what you feel. You therefore need to accept that your life has become an illusion, and by searching deeply for the truth, you will be able to reattach to reality. From an experiential point of view, we are what we feel; so given the state of our conditioning we must accept that the foundation of our whole life is an illusion.

> Our learning is our foundation, but it is only a platform from which to explore beyond, not to be limited by.

The loop of unsolvable disturbance

If the mind receives information that triggers fear, it uses this as a guide to decide what course of action it should take. If one feels fear then we interpret this as a bad feeling, and therefore create a negative association with the thing we perceive to have triggered this fear. The Problem-Solving Mind is built to remove us from anything that feels bad. This can lead to great confusion if this process is in conflict with the belief structure that the Problem-Solving Mind has previously built.

A belief structure is created to give us a sense of knowing and identity, to help us find a life that matches our beliefs in order to feel secure. However, if as a child we absorb information from an environment that has an element of familiarity to it, we may falsely associate this to mean security (even if the environment is in fact extraordinarily unhealthy and dangerous to our existence). We may find ourselves with a program or belief structure that leads us to make decisions in our interpretation of life, which create dynamics that end up making us feel bad.

Now we really have a dilemma.

The Problem-Solving Mind becomes very confused as it is guided by its own creation, its belief structure, but at the same time it is also programmed very strongly to remove itself from anything that feels bad. As the belief structure's functioning is the stronger of these two realities, we quite often stay in unhealthy situations. We live with these bad feelings in the false hope that somehow this situation will keep us safe, and that we will eventually feel good. Of course, we are relying on a false notion and our perceptions are misguiding us. Our belief structure was created without integrity and so we find ourselves repeatedly going from one situation of disturbance to another, never understanding why this happens, why we can't feel good and the nature of our self-destructive existence.

The Problem-Solving Mind experiences such a massive dilemma over these kinds of scenarios. It sees such a conflict of interest between its belief structure, which functions more on a subconscious level, and its conscious state of trying to avoid bad feelings. The 'bad' news is we are all living out a version of the above scenario.

So no matter what we do, or what our learning is, we will end up circling back to where we started; hence the journey of life into The Insanity of Humanity.

Prince or pauper?

To expand on the above discussion; if you were offered the opportunity to have your life all over again and the options were to be a prince or pauper, which would you choose?

Now for the perceptually unfortunate answer to this question.

Whether you are a prince or a pauper, if the Problem-Solving Mind controls your life you will never be satisfied.

Don't be too concerned about the nature of the journey of your life, where you were born, or what opportunities were afforded to you. Ultimately it adds up to the same thing when we are housed in the Construct.

On the other side of the coin, this observable factor in the functioning of our Constructs also opens up our minds to realise that our life story is irrelevant. Not in a dismissive sense, but in a freeing one. Any situation allows us the possibility, with the right guidance and awareness, to move beyond these restrictive parameters. In reality none is better than any other, because ultimately we end up feeling the same thing - trapped and confused within the limitations of our own thoughts.

Freedom can only happen when we realise that it is all in our mind. Once something has been experienced it is gone in a real sense. It can now only exist in the framework of our fear if we buy into the illusion that it is us. Stop and think about this - if you buy into thinking that something is you then your life will never be able to move beyond that. Hence the process of incarceration that we have created for ourselves from the day we were born.

PHASE FOURTEEN

Thoughts, emotions and survival

All emotions we currently experience are a part of our survival process. They are an expression of our fear in an attempt to create responses from the external world that will hopefully work in our favour. Our emotions are created from our thoughts. Effectively they are one and the same thing, but we get caught up in the process of constantly responding to our emotions with more problem-solving thoughts. This brings out more emotions as if it wasn't an original thought that created the emotion in the first place. We get trapped in this eternal process of thinking and responding in a desperate attempt to find security and happiness.

When thinking of emotions think of survival, hence the importance of not letting them guide the entirety of our existence - well at least not until we have stirred our deeper levels of awareness from its slumber.

Try this in spite of nature's intention!

I know feelings are powerful forces, but always remember they are just feelings. Feelings that disable us are triggered when a thought gets lost inside the Construct, and the Construct will do whatever it can to stop this thought from escaping. This also means *we* can escape as we can travel through thought – we can see life in a more expansive way every time we allow ourselves to feel and explore disturbing emotions. So for now think of thought as the space ship and feelings as the energy that can either control us, or can be used to travel to the outer reaches of existence. Hence why I encourage people to feel more, to feel everything. Otherwise you will never see life, just your own thoughts – and who needs that?

Collateral damage and the Pinhole Theory reviewed.

Beliefs are not real in the sense that they are not what we think they are. Even if we grab every single belief we have and combine it with all of the information we have acquired in our lifetime, it still only equates to a very small amount of information - particularly when you explore this idea relative to the truth of how many factors actually create all we see. A belief only represents a very minute portion of what is and it does not take into account the complex array of factors that combine to create the outcomes that we experience. Beliefs simply lead to the need to hold specific aspects of life accountable for what we see, as they work within what the mind considers to be a fairly fixed and finite reality. Of course, in the truth of life, nothing is fixed and nothing is finite. Beliefs are mechanisms of functioning serving the basic survival needs of a child, or a creature such as a wolf. The stakes are getting higher all of the time and the justifications are as obscene as ever. We are taking the acceptance of collateral damage to a new level of illness as we accept the death of innocent people and animals in order to maintain control.

Fear is the guide

The Problem-Solving Mind's survival mechanism uses the level of fear it feels as its primary guide to its decision-making. Therefore, it makes sense that it must constantly be in a state of alertness to danger. Even if you are in a situation that is primarily danger free, in fact even if it is a wonderful situation with total comfort and luxury surrounding you, the Problem-Solving Mind is still active. It is still using up large amounts of energy to function and it is still creating an underlying feeling of something not being quite right.

If the Problem-Solving Mind perceives that the external world is where all of the threats to its existence come from, it will never

PHASE FOURTEEN

fully trust anything. So no matter what surroundings you are in, it can never fully relax. Even if people learn how to remove themselves from seeing life as a problem (through processes like meditation), the Construct is still active and is still draining them of energy. In fact, its alertness is even greater now that it has been left alone in the dark.

PHASE FIFTEEN

Cold Case Files

PHASE FIFTEEN

Everything we need to know already exists within our own minds.

Collectively we just don't know it yet.

Opening the files

All of life's secrets are waiting to be discovered inside the very structure in which we are housed. If we open our eyes beyond the parameters of control that are enforced by the Problem-Solving Mind, we could permanently allow the information of life to illuminate our existence. There is no end to this process, so the restrictive sensation imposed by the Construct would no longer exist.

The human species has been attempting to understand the nature of existence for many thousands of years. We have created many interesting beliefs about the nature of what we are experiencing, however these have not changed the nature of how we experience life because we house these notions in Pain's Domain. And it is in how we experience life that determines how we respond to it.

I would suggest that it is not necessary to keep reopening the cold case files on the processes of understanding life, other than for the purpose of knowing what does not work. One opening and one analysis is adequate. Yet all I see is the continuing regurgitation of what the human mind has been aware of and has attempted to implement throughout the history of civilisation.

The programs of thoughts and emotional responses that we have been experiencing throughout the history of our existence have brought to life the possibility for us to be communicating on topics such as this. However these methods of survival are no longer adequate for humanity to rely on anymore.

Living in the 'now'

Evolution did not just create one type of human being in the hope it would survive; it created various versions with different intellectual, emotional and creative thinking capabilities, all attempting to carve out their existence on this planet.

PHASE FIFTEEN

The Universe in which we exist is a constantly changing dynamic. It has presented an endless realm of challenges to all living creatures throughout the history of life on Earth. Some of our humanlike ancestors that failed to meet these challenges (to ensure their survival) were living in the 'now'!

They had no need for the past or the future and simply responded to life as it presented itself. As peaceful a headspace that this would have allowed them to exist in, it did not allow for expansion of their imagination, nor the ability to predict and determine the future. They would not have been able to put the necessary measures in place to compensate for things such as changes in environmental conditions, let alone explore the true depth of human emotions.

For us to consider that we should travel back to such a headspace seems almost ludicrous and nonsensical, for it excludes one essential process of thought:

The ability to ask 'what if?'

If we are constantly living in the 'now', then we will never ask 'what if?' This is a question that poses concern for the future, the present, or an analysis of past events. It is the injection of awareness into our imagination that could drive us towards finding a new way to utilise the power of our minds.

I have found it intriguing to observe the large number of people that talk about living in the *now* and living in the *moment*. Living in the 'now' implies living life with no connection to the concept of a past or future; in other words, no concept of time! This is fine as time is an illusion of sorts anyway. However, the very nature of the words that we are using to describe this process defies its very existence, for what is 'now'?

Which 'now' are we talking about, the one that just went by, or the next one, or the one after that?

'Now' is still a parameter of time, at least as far as the Problem-Solving Mind is concerned. And it is the Problem-Solving Mind we are trying to teach to function in a new manner. To negate the past and the future in a conceptual sense is totally unnecessary for the development of awareness. Let's face it, we are an accumulation of all our past experiences and we don't need to remove ourselves from that. All we need to do is absorb the truth of the whole experience, not just the edited portions pertaining to our life story and our Construct. Without our past, we would not have a point of comparison as to whether the 'now' is working for us or not. Without our imagination beyond the 'now' we would not bother to try and change it anyway - like our ancestors that perished! It is a matter of not getting lost in past memories or some notion of happiness in the future, but rather embracing all aspects of our existence, and all energies and mechanisms that influence this.

What I am proposing may be more challenging than hiding in the 'now' and maybe even less pleasant, however, it will unleash true creative expression, awareness and compassion for all. We will no longer need to fight over our beliefs or surrender to *what is*.

Why would anyone accept what is if they were facing the truth of the dimension within which we exist?

To be in the 'now' denies this essential process of learning as it focuses on removing us from The Ego, which if you remember is really the Problem-Solving Mind. And whether we like it or not the Problem-Solving Mind is the thing that allows us to experience life in the first place.

> **Being in the 'now' is not real as such...**
>
> **It is actually a place or notion created by the Problem-Solving Mind to lure us into a dark place cleverly disguised as light.**

PHASE FIFTEEN

Try not to be threatened by this if you are an ardent follower of theories such as 'living in the now'. I am suggesting that we look a little deeper into what is happening. Anything that sells happiness is simply another false lure that represents what we have always been chasing in a different disguise. We are so desperate to feel good that we can even be enticed into believing that there is some *secret* to life whereby we could all find what we want! How could that be possible? And how could that do anything but feed the pathways that blind us to the needs of others. For if one embraces that they are the whole experience, then wanting anything becomes irrelevant in an obsessive sense; and in helping others we help ourselves because we are all on this journey together.

Why am I so sure about this?

Chasing happiness fits perfectly into the parameters of the Construct and it also allows integrity to be absent. Without integrity, we will never embrace the truth of what we have become as a species. My advice is that we look honestly at the darkness before we focus on the light, as it is in the darkness that we are lost. The 'good' is easy to sit in, but that does not take away the ugliness that we disguise behind our denial. To learn how to be in the 'now', which is ultimately about feeling good, will rob you of the chance to understand what you are and what it is that is driving humanity down a hideous pathway of cruelty and destruction.

Being in the 'now', with the Problem-Solving Mind so advanced in its progression through creation is nothing short of ludicrous. Our minds are not built to live in such a mode – otherwise we already would be. We need to be exploring philosophies that expand from where we currently are, as opposed to retreating back into a way of being that never worked anyway . . . a place of existence that did not allow for true compassion beyond self.

Really think about what I am saying. Being a 'good' person is not one of the essential qualities attached to being in the 'now'. It still seems to allow for value judgements of convenience and it could also be seen as quite self-indulgent. Although I am sure many people would argue with me on that – and I encourage that, as long as it is for the purpose of creating more awareness guiding us to the truth.

You don't have to be a good person to feel good - and you don't have to feel good to be a good person!

It takes a lot more strength, courage and wisdom to stay living in the pain that the Problem-Solving Mind creates rather than trying to escape it. But first we need to understand our Problem-Solving Mind otherwise how could we ever hope to teach it. In fact how would we know what to teach it? I say this in light of the fact that our minds are a clear representation of life on this planet - creating everything we are attempting to remove ourselves from.

If we would really like to test the nature of our character, then observe how we treat other living things under the following four circumstances:

1. When we are not obliged to acknowledge the cruelty attached to our behaviour.
2. When we are not obliged to treat something with decency.
3. When we are not getting what we want.
4. When we are not feeling good.

Being in the 'now' does not necessarily lead to a person satisfying the above criteria, even though it may lead to a sensation of contentment. Any journey of the mind and the spirit that does not take us deeper into the truth, the truth of the pain that drives our lives and the truth of the suffering that we are creating all around us, is of little worth. It represents nothing but another carrot being dangled in our faces to take advantage of our fears.

I strongly sense that focusing on awareness embodies more honesty than focusing on the 'now'. To be functioning with higher levels of awareness does not necessitate being attached to the 'now', even though it does open up a portal to a version of it should we so choose to travel there. In fact, I would go as far as suggesting that being in the 'now' in its purest form may actually negate the lateral potential of awareness – hence destroying our connection to true creativity with compassion.

'Now' versus 'What If'

I have devoted much of this book to explaining the 'what if' pathway of our human ancestors. In essence it represents the functioning of the Problem-Solving Mind. I am sure by now that you can clearly see that this pathway, like living in the 'now', also appears to have an end.

So is that it for us? Are we living on borrowed time?

Is it inevitable that we will not survive?

That depends on you. That depends on me. That depends on everyone and their ability to function beyond whatever it is that we have previously relied upon in order to survive.

The possibility is alive. The commitment is questionable.

At this phase in our development as a species, many religions and spiritual practices have arisen to master how to live in the 'now'. To some degree I would say they have been quite successful, however, I don't see true freedom of emotional expression and individuality within the ranks of the devoted followers. In fact, much doubt is raised in my mind about why such strict regiment and conformity is present, or even necessary within such a supposed place of peaceful serenity. For if people were truly living in such a place in their minds then there would be no need for any routines. The fact that they have routines indicates planning, controls and a form of strategic management. These attributes are interestingly those that I would attribute to the functioning of the Problem-Solving Mind without Conscious Awareness!

This is why I am proposing, that in an evolutionary sense, we are from a line of genetic engineering that was never built to be in the 'now'. This is why we cannot maintain it and inject it into a system of functioning. There may be unique individuals who have brains that have diverged from the norm, thus allowing them to function in a more simplistic enlightened fashion - however I truly doubt even that.

Even if you don't agree with any of my philosophies on the Problem-Solving Mind and the Construct, there is still much evidence which is hard to dispute, pointing to the fact that we are incapable of employing techniques like living in the 'now'. However, there is an essence that can be extracted from the concept of living in the 'now' which can be injected into the pathway which we have been previously locked into - the 'what if' pathway.

Living in Isness

So let's explore the merger of these two pathways of thinking.

I strongly recommend that we forget trying to meditate or medicate ourselves into a state of eternal happiness, whether it is via the pathways of religion, spiritual practices or popping a pill. It is 'time' to face what we have for so long avoided - the pain that is guiding our systems of functioning. Through a process of deep lateral and open awareness, we can transform our lives by first accepting and understanding what is. This allows for connection to every aspect of our experience: the past, present and future, including the good, the bad and the ugly!

We can't change the brain that we are within but we can change the way we use it. I would suggest that the most important thing that we could be focusing on right 'now' is to understand the energy that is driving our minds. It is not about denouncing pain from our minds, but rather going deeper into an understanding of it and the effects it has on our behaviour. Until we clearly understand the Problem-Solving Mind and find a way to teach it and guide it, everything we create and every philosophy we develop about life, will simply be a manifestation of fear within the confines of the Construct.

Facing and observing our deep painful responses to life contains the possibility of unleashing our inner strength. Not just the pain withheld in our life story but the pain being experienced all around us. If the pain is there and we are not feeling it, then this is evidence that we are not fully experiencing life and are therefore not fully experiencing Isness.

By not identifying with our emotions, yet still allowing for the free expression of them, we allow for the process of turning pain into wisdom. It is an amazing thing to experience when we see pain as information rather than something to fear. Life is then a constant process of learning and growing, hence the older we get the wiser we get.

Explore life but try not to see it as a problem. Otherwise we will just create the same sensations of fear in a different disguise of potential happiness. Don't waste any time working out how to love 'you' either. Just be aware and give love. What we give determines what we can receive. We can be in pain and still give love, rather than going too deep into introspection.

I am suggesting a journey that is very different to embracing the illusionary cold case theories from the past and the resurgence of them into 'now'. They are not unsolved mysteries, just theories that were created by the Construct for the purpose of keeping us in the Construct. These theories are doing nothing but digging us deeper into the illusion that we are all trapped in. It does not matter what we do in the Construct, as it fulfils the parameters to keep The Game of life in motion.

This game ultimately is not a problem that we can solve, but that is how we currently look at it.

> Rather than playing The Game that is presented by our emotional states, we should stop and understand the nature of The Game before we become The Game!

The key is not to run and hide from pain to a state of bliss. We don't have to be happy to have integrity and compassion, and it is only these qualities that will save us.

Integrity is the truth of everything and it is the essence of Isness. It is awareness and compassionate expansive thinking that will get us there; awareness that looks beyond the parameters of The Game, beyond fear, beyond beliefs and beyond the Construct. Hence unleashing the potential of our minds whereby a new version of problem-solving is waiting.

> A technique that the mind cannot currently conceptualise, but can learn to trust.

Awareness in the Construct is only useful when we know that we are in it in the first place. In knowing this we can also stay in it to observe it and understand it. This piece of machinery in which we exist has so much undeveloped potential it is phenomenal – and thank goodness it can only be unleashed when a person steps into a complete place of compassion. Otherwise the consequences would be devastating.

Emotions

In the Construct every emotion is an expression of pain.

> Pain can be glorious, hideous and anywhere in between on this emotional spectrum.

It is all one masterfully designed system. Emotions exist for the purpose of survival and evolution; including love. The more powerful beautiful emotions keep us continually searching for more in this realm. We never want to leave this dimension as we are programmed to believe that happiness is close at hand, not realising that these more enjoyable emotions are also just an expression of pain. It looks like we need to get to know pain a lot more intimately, as in reality we can't run from it. Even living in the 'now' exacerbates this issue, as this is just a temporary solution.

How could we leave if we don't know where we are?

Unless of course we are relying on luck - it is not possible! Why? Because the dimension we are in is too well designed to incarcerate consciousness.

If we truly see the potential for a life beyond our existing connection with pain, then I recommend we stop running away from it and spend more time trying to understand it. It is through our repressed emotions that we create the impulse to run. Emotions in a damaged state can be a very confusing obstacle to finding Isness.

Being in the Isness is spiritual in its sensation but intellectual in its awareness. The mind is certainly not left alone in the dark. In fact it is right there with us, jointly embracing the truth of everything.

Truth is the only valuable commodity – and denial is the only thing that is traded to get it.

A reasonable trade off wouldn't you say?

Of course, it is not a trade at all, as once we are truly aware denial does not exist.

Isness is not a state of permanent happiness, but rather one of depth and richness in our hearts where the sensation of the real us lives. If we are in Isness then our deeper levels of awareness and compassion are alive. And when alive we could do nothing but stop and help anything in need, we could not eat another living and feeling creature, and we could not knowingly partake in any cruelty at all.

It is about experiencing every aspect of human emotions and allowing life to present all that needs to be embraced. It supersedes the process of wanting, as life could not be any fuller than it is. So our learning and wisdom is open to the Universe to absorb all that crosses our path. There is no need to go looking for anything in an insatiable sense, yet it is still possible to open portals to our imagination.

It is like going with the flow but with a mind that is more attuned, has more available energy, more clarity, more available intelligence and more compassion for life.

Isness is found when our reality is expanding as opposed to life in the Construct, which is one of ongoing retraction. Expansiveness opens portals to transcend beyond this physical dimension, while still allowing for Conscious Awareness to stay right in the midst of evolution where our true salvation lies. It allows for the deepest of emotional experiences with awareness attached to it. In this instance our emotions can never take over our lives and we always know we are not them in a restrictive sense. Instead we expand thought and feelings to expand ourselves.

Is it about always feeling good?

No it isn't! Not yet anyway

It is a sensation of permanent connectedness to a place of deeper awareness. Our strength is always there when we need it, which gives us the courage to voyage into our pain and beyond - to keep diving back in as life unfolds. It allows us to put our integrity before our existing survival pathway, a pathway where we will sacrifice just about anything to maintain some distorted notion of self.

PHASE FIFTEEN

Imagine if...

Imagine if we all started to feel the true energy of our planet — good or bad

Think how this would change our experience of life and our corresponding actions. It is not about wallowing in our own fears and insecurities — but rather understanding them, setting ourselves free of them and then grabbing this wisdom and strength so we can feel the truth of our global reality.

Then and only then will we ever be able to face and deal with what we have created on this planet.

> **Living an expansive life is about feeling to learn... rather than learning to feel.**

This also equates to having so much more to give and therefore this cycle of life keeps building. Imagine if we were all doing this? That is, sharing Isness, expansiveness, integrity and truth, rather than distorted pain, fear, lies, manipulation and control.

Isness has layers of depth of connectedness. The beautiful quality that exists within this process is that there is no denial about the true nature of our being.

> **It is less about doing and more about being.**

Yet oddly it opens up the portals for being more productive and creative than ever, depending on the Isness of what life is presenting. In Isness we don't 'do' for the sake of 'doing' — that is obsessive behaviour driven by fear.

In Isness, we will be comfortable with whether we are busy or inactive, because we will see truth in all aspects of functioning. The obsession for happiness and achievement, that we can see our minds demanding, is no longer driving our existence and we teach our mind to see beyond this simplistic and blinkered manner of existing. So life is no longer obsessed with outcomes, although we would be aware that they occur perceptually in the ongoing cycle of life.

In the Isness we would allow ourselves to be humble to others' energies and all that this encompasses. This does not mean we would always like what we are experiencing, but we would have broken free of the need to run from bad feelings towards good ones. We would be interested in understanding what is causing our disturbance or happiness. Everything in our life would make sense in some shape or form, so this would always lead to growth and enhanced learning.

Imagine living a life where we felt pain, but no longer needed to run away from it.

Imagine enjoying the riches of life's experiences without the need for self-serving happiness.

Imagine living with integrity such that the consequences of our actions were not just understood, but also full of compassion for all of life.

Imagine living on a planet and being part of the growth of a species that never knowingly or unnecessarily destroyed another living being.

> Imagine living a life where we could actually live with ourselves!

Opening up our sixth sense

We all have the ability to develop our Sixth Sense once we embrace Isness.

When awareness is at the forefront of our existence, our five senses receive information and open up our sixth sense. We then channel all this to the Problem-Solving Mind while bypassing the editing process.

PHASE FIFTEEN

Now we are no longer in the Construct.

To clarify; we collect life's information from our five senses. This can then be channelled instantly through our Conscious Awareness, hence creating our Sixth Sense. Life's information is then sent directly into our minds and guess what we experience?

Ourselves!

As this information is unedited it contains no fear, allowing us to maintain our integrity, whatever the sensation we are experiencing. We do not lose our emotions, as that is part of the human journey and part of our experience in the processes of creation and evolution. What is removed from this new equation in our lives is the constant feeling of confusion. When we are confused we will be aware of that too, so it won't be long before we aren't confused anymore.

Being aware incorporates acknowledging that we don't know everything, which really means we don't know anything! Meaning, as soon as we know something life has already permanently changed. So don't waste any more time getting to know whom you are, as in reality that is ever-changing.

Think about that for a while.

You would never get bored being you!

This is the point to kick start awareness and then our task is to keep it alive. Allowing awareness to exist in front of our emotions while at the same time not denying their expression. Emotions hold a world of knowing once they are understood and not solely held in the world of pain and fear.

To experience life via our sixth sense is to truly experience life.

Unified self

When our sixth sense is alive, we have the opportunity to experience the Unified Self.

This is a place of existence where there would no longer be any separation between the functioning of our minds and our Conscious Awareness. The merger would be complete.

Life would no longer be seen as a problem that needs solving. Therefore we would have the potential to not just flow with life, but to realise that we are life, so the need to categorise and separate all that we experience would dissolve in a controlling sense. It is in this process of categorisation that we allow for the application of integrity by convenience.

The Unified Self cannot be found through a process of meditation or traditional spiritual practices. These techniques may help a person to acquire momentary sensations of peacefulness at the cost of removing awareness from the mind. The longer the Problem-Solving Mind is detached from awareness, the more power and corruption it creates within its thinking, and this is what we would be returning to.

Creating our Unified Self requires powering up the mind rather than trying to relax it. It is about injecting it with all of life's information via our Sixth Sense – not just the bits that we want to see!

Life Speed Synchronisation

Evolution is occurring at a certain speed.

When I use the term speed in this instance, just think of it as nothing more than a concept to aid in the process of sensing what I am describing. Life is travelling at a speed that requires no measurement and certainly does not need to be controlled.

PHASE FIFTEEN

The Unified Self can experience our journey through evolution at Life Speed.

We are currently weighing our minds down with the burden of problem-solving. Within the confines of our Construct, life is travelling faster than we can manage to track it, hence the desire to control it. In fact in our current mode of existence, we are totally at odds with life as we attempt to structure it within a process of beliefs. Beliefs are only created for the purpose of maintaining life in defined parameters within our mind, rather than flowing with it.

Once we truly open up to the concept of there being a Sixth Sense and the possibility of creating a Unified Self, we will be able to synchronise our minds at the same speed life is travelling. This removes the abrasive feeling of trying to impose something that life simply cannot embrace.

At Life Speed we become life.

We become one.

To feel this is like being supercharged with intelligence. Then and only then we can truly transcend this dimension by creating another. Hence we have now become creators rather than reactors!

I have deliberately not elaborated on these potential pathways of existence. I do not want the focus of attention to be on these possibilities, as they will become outcomes that we need to attain. Then we will never get there, as outcomes represent destinations that we attempt to problem-solve our way towards.

For now it is enough that we just become aware of the mechanisms that are keeping us captive, hence why I have devoted most of this book to that topic. The rest will follow when ready.

PHASE SIXTEEN

Awareness - science or magic?

PHASE SIXTEEN

Awareness may not give us the life we want, but it will give us a life we can live with.

Awareness is freedom

When I am aware, I can feel that I am functioning such that my thoughts and emotions are connected to, but not determined by my beliefs.

I think of this attachment as more like an invisible energy that flows in and around my mind, rather than something that has been created for the purpose of controlling my decisions and limiting my freedom.

When I am in a complete state of awareness I experience the sensation of being the observer of life while fully connected to it all at the same time. Think of this place not as something that has defined boundaries, but as something that allows me to be free to explore my existence to wherever the chemistry of the connection between life and me travels.

While functioning in this realm I am absorbing and experiencing all of the information that life is presenting, rather than just the bits and pieces that my mind extracts from life in order to make its fear based decisions.

> **Awareness in an expansive state guides the journey of existence through the truth into a world of realistic possibilities.**

The more aware I am, the more I am able to absorb the information of life for the purpose of giving rather than for the greed-driven processes of wanting and control.

Awareness creates

Awareness is the key ingredient in the journey of my life beyond the Insanity of Humanity; a right of passage that will build structural integrity in my mind while also bringing courage, passion, emotional depth, empathy, honesty, purpose and Isness into my existence.

Awareness creates a life that I may not like owing to the reality of what I see in this world, however it allows me to understand and embrace it as it takes away the confusion that is felt when I buy into the illusion of choice. It gives me the opportunity to live beyond humanity's existing realm of misunderstood pain and all of the distorted pathways that it manifests. At the very least it allows me to live in the pain without corrupting my journey, in fact it inspires me to go deeper into understanding what is and what could be.

Awareness creates a mind for me to travel in that will bring life to the essence of me, rather than a fear-based version.

> Awareness stimulates the metamorphic processes into a new phase of human evolution.

The science of awareness is magic!

Is there a definable methodology that can be observed and practised on the journey of awareness, or is it something that you do, and then let the magic begin?

> It's a bit of both!

The science of awareness, for the purpose of this discussion, can be considered as the knowledge and understanding of the systematic processes that lead to awareness. So from this point of view, I would suggest that although I can definitely share with you the science behind the journey to awareness, it still has a powerful sense of magic embodied in the process. There are many aspects to the effects of it that are mysterious and extraordinary. That is the experience of truly sensing the permanent state of Newness that our Universe functions in.

Awareness - science or magic?

Everything that I have discovered about the human journey has come from the sometimes simple, sometimes beautiful, sometimes complicated, sometimes sad, and sometimes joyful process of expanding my reality within an aware state of being.

> Awareness creates a journey with a deep sense of truth.
>
> It creates a life I can live with even if I cannot change what I see.

My journey of awareness

To help you explore this beautiful topic, I would like to share some small glimpses of my personal journey to give you a taste of who I am as a person. To help you see that each aspect of the knowledge and truth that I have acquired has come from freely expressing my feelings to maintain a state of expansive awareness.

Since I can remember, I have been extremely attuned to the mechanisms of human behaviour and the belief structures that individuals and society have attempted to impose on each other, themselves, and me. I sensed these beliefs had been created through a process of fear - not wisdom. This awareness explained why I always had a feeling of being controlled; a feeling that everyone around me was creating their identity via the information of life they were being presented with – particularly by other people. I always sensed the potential for corruption if one was to define their existence in such a manner, as it relies so heavily on trusting that the information you are being presented with is honest and pertaining to your best interests as an individual. Which it is not – it is all founded on lies!

I witnessed most people were absorbing the nature of their environment whether it had anything to do with who they actually were. For example, just because I was growing up in Australia, it did not really make sense to me why nearly everybody I knew identified him or herself as an Australian. As if that had something to do with whom they were. I could obviously see that where I grew up had a big influence on the experiences of my life; however, I never thought it had anything to do with whom I actually was. I saw the information of life beyond the superficial beliefs and meanings that were being presented to me, and this is because I was fortunate enough to have grown up in an environment where I could nurture my awareness hence allowing my reality to continually expand.

I always felt like there were two aspects to my existence: one that was interacting with life in order to develop some sense of my place in the world, and a second self that was observing the whole process from a place of deep purity and compassion. This awareness led me to create a journey that offered a high level of truth, emotional depth, individuality and connectedness with life. In opposition to this, the system created by people was attempting to mould me into a world of 'should do this' and 'should do that'. A world of wanting, control, achievement and success - a world of nothing but outcomes and more confusion waiting at each destination arrival point.

My journey led me to develop my knowledge and knowing of the real self and the artificial self - and how these two forces could influence the individual behaviour of people and the development of systems that they existed in. I was starting to sense the multidimensional realities of life that were creating the Universe that I was experiencing in my mind.

In my childhood, dreams had a great impact on my awareness. I was subconsciously sensing the different energies that existed within people and my dreams communicated this into my Conscious Awareness. These dreams were a big feature in my life for some time and they initially led to an attachment of fear and confusion. However, I was determined as my life progressed to understand what I was sensing. I therefore explored these observations beyond my dream states, to find the source of these visions within the world in which I was interacting.

This sense of knowing that all is not quite as it seems created a powerful driving force within me. To my dismay I quickly discovered that I seemed to be very alone in what I was sensing. This left me wondering to whom could I turn for support and understanding - you would not exactly have a chat with Satan if you wanted to find a way out of hell. And to me that was where we were all living, other people just didn't seem to know it! It was not hard to find evidence for feeling this way as I watched my peers pick on the weak and disadvantaged to gain some sensation of power. Even those that were not directly partaking did little to stop it. In fact, it seemed more important to be accepted by the group than to stand up for any sense of integrity or decency. Of course I did the opposite, which drew a lot of unwanted attention my way. But I accepted that if that was the consequence of being a decent caring person then so be it. Not that it made me feel good, hence why I quickly learnt that life was not about feeling good - it was about honesty!

Where have all of the wise elders gone?

Wisdom was certainly not being offered to me by the system, whether it was from my schoolteachers or from the leaders of the various systems that were in place at the time. I couldn't see how I could respect anyone or the systems they were representing, if they were to use a process of control in order for me to behave true to their wishes.

I was however very fortunate to have been blessed with wonderful parents. Although they did not have any knowledge on this topic, they always offered me a safe haven for unedited expression of my thoughts and feelings. Even here there was an element of confusion, as I could still sense this multidimensional reality within them as well. It also became apparent that this artificial creation within people was always present and listening whether it was exposing its face or not. It seemed to have a life of its own separate from the actual person and I could always see it. Interestingly, it rarely knew that I could sense its existence, so it seemed wise for me to keep this awareness to myself - at least until I understood what I was dealing with. So in many ways I was being faced with quite a dilemma and that left me with only one true pathway - to continue down the road of awareness alone.

I sensed there was a far more expansive pathway than control and that was the expression of truth, honesty, giving and compassion for all of life. In fact it actually seemed very obvious right from the beginning that people were trapped in some strange system of functioning, as if they were robots being true to some kind of computer program, and I knew that was not a life for me. I was sensing the existence of what I refer to today as the Construct.

Respect for all life

I honestly feel that one of the key and most important elements of life that awareness led me to (at a very early age) was to have a great appreciation for the life of all living creatures. My caring for life was not used as motivation, but rather as an observation that I happily let affect the entirety of my journey. It occurred to me that if you see your own existence as more important than anything else, then you would stay trapped in a very basic and blinkered mode of existence. Stuck in a journey that would have disallowed me from receiving the true extent of what experiences are possible.

This would therefore leave me with nothing but a distorted sense of self to give to the world. What the Universe gives you back when you are in this mode goes without saying. I also learnt that people were inadvertently, through a process of greed and control, robbing themselves of opening an incredible gift - the journey of being Consciously Aware and emotionally honest.

As a boy I used to find it strange, that while I was putting so much effort into saving anything, from an insect through to a lost dog, many other boys were blindly on a pathway to destroy life as if they found some kind of pleasure in it. This destructive behaviour that I witnessed caused me great pain and suffering, yet it was this awareness and the emotions that it stimulated, which created the drive for me to understand the mechanisms of life. It inspired the desire to see if there was a way that we could move beyond the obsessive process of control that people seemed to be trapped in.

Looking back as an adult, I can see these children simply lacked an awareness of their existence and they were being true to the basic and primitive programs that have flowed through the DNA pathways of life for millions of years to this day. However, the difference with humans compared to other animals is twofold; firstly in humans these programmed behaviours are being channelled through a construct of belief systems that are corrupt and have no structural integrity, and secondly, humans not only have the ability to observe their own behaviour, but they also have the ability to enjoy the suffering they create – hence the dangerous possibilities attached to the cyber realities of the mind when guided by pain.

An honest realisation I had to come to was the fact that all of these human characteristics that exist in other people also existed in me. It was just my awareness that ensured they were expressed through a process of integrity rather than control. So whatever state of existence I am in, I am always aware, therefore always learning and growing intellectually and spiritually.

Awareness allows me to continue flowing rather than feeling like I am stuck at some point in time. The more aware I become, the more I see the truth of life, rather than some narrow and basic perspective of it. So in the nature of this mode of functioning, I am able to experience all aspects of life, without taking it personally – although I do regularly slip and catch myself reacting, so I stop, look at it, feel it and grab the learning from it. Hence for me I have discovered the ultimate state of observation to allow for the ongoing expression and evolution of the Conscious Energy that lives inside all living beings.

PHASE SIXTEEN

Caged in a world of control and pain

Although I was aware of the processes that led to the creation of my belief structure, I still had to learn to understand that while housed in this system, awareness would still encompass a great deal of pain and emotional disturbance.

The pain that I experienced as I watched the apparently thoughtless and sometimes utterly cruel behaviour of my fellow human beings towards each other and all living creatures alike, started to accumulate within me as the years of my youth went by. I could sense and recognise within myself that this pain was creating a disturbed, sad, tough and angry version of me. This pain, like I could see in other people, was starting to develop a life of its own as it attempted to control my decisions in life.

However, despite the deep and sometimes confusing roller coaster ride of human emotions I was experiencing, awareness ensured that the journey of my life stayed founded in integrity. By integrity I do not mean perfect behaviour as there is no such thing, but rather I could be honest about my actions hence continuing the process of expanding my mind's awareness.

I may not have always got what I wanted out of life, but I always clearly knew at any moment how I arrived at the destination to which I found myself. I knew this made more sense to me than the other selfish pathways that society was offering, like achievement and success.

Integrity brings to your life whatever it does, for if you devote your life to trying to get what you want, you will always have to compromise your integrity. For me, if that is what achievement is all about, then you can have it. In some ways, I unwittingly created a journey into the realm of integrity and compassion right from the beginning. However, it wasn't long before I became aware of this and then realised the importance of becoming aware in general. I soon discovered that awareness was an infinite journey of learning, for as you create awareness of new awareness, this leads to more awareness and so on it goes.

> Awareness is a self-propelled energy and all you have to do is jump on board!

Can awareness be lonely?

All this talk of waking up and becoming consciously evolved sounds great - but let's keep this all real. It is not all fun and good times no matter how aware or emotionally evolved you are. Also, the pathway to these places is not easily found, or we would have walked right into the arms of it a long time ago.

My journey led me to feel extremely lonely at times, especially when I felt the need to stop the destructive behaviours of other human beings. This only served to create a sensation of separation of me versus them. Awareness then continued to allow me to see that to fuel this train of thought was futile and purposeless. I knew it would simply become another example of the struggle that is being witnessed in the journey of our species since recorded times. That is, the struggle of one belief structure against another.

It wasn't long before I realised that to try and stop people's appetite for destruction was only a very temporary solution. If anything, it seemed to have the overall effect of feeding more fear and anger into the situation I was responding to, hence fuelling the process of pain not wisdom.

So although I could see I had created beliefs about life and everything in it, I did not let these beliefs totally define who I was or my actions. However, I did ensure that my beliefs were created with structural integrity combined with lateral flexibility.

Because of this awareness, I realised that to partake in any process that simply focused on outcomes and on trying to create an opposing force to what did not seem right, would only lead to more confusion - both within myself and within those that I would challenge. This left me with a very clear direction for my life and that was to understand the science of life, to embrace the magic of life, to find an alternative way of functioning, to share this with the world and then to accept that what will be will be.

Compare this to how the government representatives in your country share their views on how you should behave. Ultimately it gets down to 'do it or else!' How could we possibly get 'wise' if that is the energy that blankets our thinking, thus determining our behaviour and corresponding actions. In a state of true awareness nobody could endorse or enforce such an attitude, hence we would interact through understanding not enforced controls.

Enter the Problem-Solving Mind

I always sensed it was important to let the deeper truth that awareness led me to, be the guide for my life, rather than letting the simple process of running away from bad feelings and running towards good feelings determine the nature of my existence.

In understanding this, I developed an awareness of the existence of the Problem-Solving Mind as the creator of my beliefs (the Construct) and of all the human behaviour that was questionable at the very least. Then it soon became apparent that if there is a Construct, there must be something outside of the Construct - and there is. So again through processes of deep awareness, I embarked on a journey into a new realm of existence that I had never experienced but sensed was there.

Over the period of my life until now, on many occasions I explored beyond the confines of the artificial reality in the Construct. This new place of existence I had discovered almost defies description within the intellectual realm; it really is a place of magic!

In this realm everything makes sense, it is infinite yet it is not, as there is no restrictive sense of time but only an awareness of it. It is separate from the physical realm, yet it encompasses everything around it and between it.

It is a world of existence that I can peacefully enter without needing to return. So I knew, because of this observation, I was functioning separately from the excessive and insatiable realm of the traditional human thought.

Interestingly, this awareness led me to see that the journey for my existence was not to spend my life trying to stay out of the Construct, but conversely to have the courage to stay in it. If I am going to be in it, knowing that there is more, it made sense to understand the nature of its functioning with this new and deep sense of my existence.

> Awareness is a process of life - a necessary component in the Journey of uniting with the Human Mind.
>
> The creation of a Unified Self.

Let the adventure begin

I would like to say I personally love there being a sense of magic about life. Embracing the unknown can create an exciting and adventurous journey, as you become a pioneer in your field of endeavour expressed through the uniqueness of your being. For no matter how much I discover, or learn to understand about life and everything in it, it is always new. The excitement of life is forever present and never boring. It also made an interesting challenge to write this book as I have new ideas and philosophies every day.

I also find solace in knowing that whether I fully understand something or not, the truth is always out there to be found or created. My awareness of this inspires me rather than scares me. So I am willing to embrace the unknown, as life is permanently unknown as it is always new. Once we become aware of this we have the potential to move into Life Speed Synchronisation, a place where the mind and life function simultaneously, allowing for expansion of ones own reality yet still founded on the unedited truth of life's information. So learning is not at the mercy of time anymore, as you and life have become one harmonious entity.

When this journey of passion is pursued from outside of the Problem-Solving Mind's existing restrictions, in a state of intelligent and enlightened awareness, the process of science and magic almost feel like one harmonious entity. I would strongly suggest that we never buy into the thought of needing to know everything, as this is the insatiable journey of the Problem-Solving Mind.

Sometimes relax and enjoy not knowing, as although this may sound strange, in many ways this is a very peaceful entry point into the process of awareness, which actually leads to knowing. In other words, try not to see life as a problem that needs solving, because if you do, you are effectively saying you are the problem.

When we are in a state of awareness our intelligence takes on a new realm of functioning, in which our thinking becomes an exciting journey of expansive, creative exploration with integrity, rather than an obsessive process of control.

When awareness is combined with patience, knowledge and knowing, it can bring itself from the world of magic into a unified existence with science. It is in fact the necessary tool to create the Unified Self, which is the evolved state of enlightenment combined in perfect harmony with the intelligence of the physical realm.

Obstacle to awareness

I have on many occasions been presented with the argument that awareness creates more pain and it would be better to remain unaware in life so you can't be hurt - hence the saying; 'Ignorance is bliss'. This false and erroneously created fear-based notion is one of the greatest obstacles you will meet on your journey to embrace awareness as a way of life.

> **These people haven't stayed around long enough to see the end of the movie!**

The movie of life is actually a never-ending one and to embrace this is to realise that to leave the movie is merely a false notion anyway. You can't leave it in reality, so sit in it until you understand it! And then who knows what is next!

Mourning the loss of beliefs

For the purpose of expanding your understanding of the concept of awareness, it is important to realise you will possibly experience and get trapped in the sensation of mourning as you go through the process of trying to let go of certain key beliefs - ones that have become central to your existence, even if they have created and continue to create undesirable outcomes.

In this instance you have mistakenly bought into the notion that these beliefs are you and hence they often affect all of your behaviour, in terms of how you feel about yourself and how you interact with the world. You have become so heavily reliant upon these beliefs for your sense of self, that to lose one or all of them would be like losing an aspect of your existence.

> **If you think that a belief is you, then for this belief to be taken away is equivalent to part of you dying.**

This may sound extreme, but for a lot of people this is exactly what they experience after the light of truth is first shone on an aspect of their beliefs. The sensation of mourning occurs because

PHASE SIXTEEN

they can consciously see the corruption in their behaviour and all that it is connected to. They realise they must let go of this aspect of their existence and usually a huge element of resistance takes over to halt this process.

If you have already developed the necessary life skills and understanding of human behaviour, then the pathways into awareness and beyond will be relatively painless and somewhat uplifting. If the process is unimpeded by distorted pain and the excessive fear that it creates, then potentially you could confidently travel down the following pathway:

1. Awareness
2. Reconciliation
3. Mourning
4. Non reactive acknowledgement
5. Wisdom

When you give yourself to this process it feels like a natural journey in the continuance of life rather than a broken down system or a list of procedural steps. Although this process sounds simple, never underestimate the power and the cunning ingenuity of the Problem-Solving Mind. Starting the process is no guarantee of finishing it, however to not start is insane! Practice makes perfect.

Increasing awareness means exposing beliefs for what they are, so initially there will be a mourning process before you let go and free the mind to a life beyond meaning.

Grief is experienced prior to letting go of a belief, whatever that belief is attached to. The stronger the belief and the more value you have attributed to the thing it is attached to, the greater the level of grief.

Letting go does not hurt, but holding on does!

Awareness - science or magic?

Awareness is like a shedding process, losing the layers of insanity until we and the mind are totally free - free of all the beliefs and false notions that we have relied on for so long to exist.

It is a process of metamorphosis, so of course it will be painful at times.

This process involves changing the structure of our mind and the nature of how it has functioned for many years. At times it feels enlightening and at others times hellish in the degree of pain that we are capable of feeling. These moments of pain are intense, but brief if we truly understand what is happening. The more we learn to apply awareness the quicker the process becomes and therefore the shorter the periods of resistance and pain.

Stay attentive to the possibility that once the Problem-Solving Mind sees this new level of awareness, it will desperately try to see if it can rebuild what was, to re-establish an old belief, or at the very least create some kind of compromise. This is the process of reconciliation.

Often the mind is trying to rebuild what was and this is just not possible. So of course we will experience great pain as the Problem-Solving Mind exhausts its resources to hold onto its illusions. Eventually the Problem-Solving Mind will give up, as it cannot find a solution and now we experience the sensation of mourning.

At this point, we feel like we have lost an aspect of our being and can find nothing to replace it with. However, if we stop identifying with this pain and realise that the beliefs and issues it is attached to are not us, we will finally find the courage to sit in a non reactive place of expansive awareness. There may be a moment of fear as you free-fall into the unknown. However, if you remain in this state of alert calmness, you will quickly feel a sense of wisdom and knowing. This creates a sensation of empowerment and strength, for in this moment you are experiencing the real you.

PHASE SIXTEEN

The real you can handle any experience because it is not lost in the experience.

You are the observer and guide and letting go allows you to flow at the speed of life. You are now free-falling without gravity! One of the keys to maintaining a journey of awareness is to ensure that you continually expand your reality, hence allowing for bigger and more dynamic emotional experiences to enter your world without overwhelming you.

Effectively you are absorbing more of life's information until one day you will have it all. This will allow you to function from a place of understanding not fear.

Is letting go cold and heartless?

For many people letting go of their deep emotional connections seems cold and heartless. It almost feels that there is integrity in attaching pain to certain situations, relationships and particularly death related experiences. I can clearly testify to the power of the mind and its desperate need to hold onto a belief that has become so deeply entrenched in the reality of our existence.

I experienced this when my father passed away and although I considered myself aware and knowledgeable of human behaviour at the time, I suffered greatly for many years. I could not let go of the structures in my mind that I had attached to his existence in order for me to feel that life was safe, secure and had meaning.

At the time, it felt cold and heartless to stop grieving for him; in fact, it even seemed honourable to remain in my pain. I do not want to suggest that what I did or what others may have done in a similar nature is wrong. I just would like to make you aware that the longer you hold on to a belief that you know is no longer yours to have, then the longer you will be in pain. You will, if you remain in that state, fall deeply into the depths of depression.

Having sat in that painful place did however afford me the possibility to see all that controlled my reality – and I looked!

Knowledge versus knowing

Knowing is knowledge that you have embraced the truth of. In this instance you no longer use this information to reinforce your belief structure

I have heard it said on many occasions that information is power.

There is some truth in this, but the power of information (knowledge) is currently in the wrong hands and being controlled by forces that do not serve our best interest.

Information simply lives in the Construct and therefore it is being used for the greater manipulation of life, which further enhances the pain and suffering that we are experiencing and globally sharing as human beings. We will continue to keep experiencing the ongoing anguish that is reminiscent of today's world, as long as we buy into this false notion that information is power. The true power lies in turning this knowledge into knowing, so it is no longer information, it is something carrying far less potential for corruption - and that is wisdom.

In knowing there are no problems.

In knowledge there is always fear and pain.

Knowledge is the phase when the Problem-Solving Mind receives and absorbs the information that life is sending to it. Therefore, knowledge is a problem that needs solving, because it is attached to the process of identifying what we want in order to feel good and to protect us from feeling bad. However, this is the necessary starting point we must not avoid as long as we are in the Construct.

Knowledge is a wonderful thing, just be careful not to misuse it, not to turn it into a problem. Don't allow the mind to keep reinforcing the prison of its perceived existence because it thinks there is danger outside. You will never feel free until you embrace the knowing of what is outside, as then you will be flowing with the reality of life rather than seeing it as something separate that you must protect yourself from.

Knowledge serves as a restrictive and limiting process in decision-making

Think about how much knowledge you would have to acquire if you wanted to know everything!

So I would suggest we all be honest with ourselves and realise whatever knowledge we currently have, no matter how highly educated we are, it is still just a minute proportion of what we could possibly know. In fact, the more educated people become in a specific area, the more narrow minded they become. Then their ability to think laterally and to live in the Truth is lost. In fact, they often attach their personal notion of self-esteem to being knowledgeable.

You can see in some people the need to acquire knowledge becomes an obsessive pathway. They believe it will make them more intelligent, more interesting and give their life more worth. Unfortunately, this need is simply limiting and restricting whatever intelligence they have and driving them deeper into their insecurities. They are trying to find strength from an incorrectly identified destination. No matter how much information you try to jam into your Construct, nothing will change the fact that it is still a psychological structure that imprisons your mind and therefore imprisons your potential.

Although I utilise the knowledge I have acquired in my life, I do not refer to it very often as I regard every situation as being totally new and different from anything I have ever experienced before. This allows me to stay open to absorbing the truth, rather than having the desire to enforce my existing knowledge on that situation in order to make myself feel better - just so I can strengthen my existing belief structure. I am not suggesting this is easy to do and sometimes I slip up, but when I do, I am aware of that fact rather than getting fooled into responding to it.

For example, as I write this book, I am not acquiring information from any one else's work and I am not consciously trying to drag information out of my existing knowledge base. I simply start writing and see what comes out trusting my knowledge will be used if necessary.

You can, if you so choose, live so that as life progresses you keep aiding the Problem-Solving Mind in the process of increasing the strength of its fortress. This represents the confines of your existence, forever increasing the quantity of things you fear in your world and therefore the amount of things you believe you need to protect yourself from. This technique, which I certainly don't recommend, is the one being employed most commonly in today's world. As life progresses this method becomes more difficult to maintain.

Stress levels increase as the need to control increases.

Just to reiterate, let's clarify what I am suggesting. Try expanding the dimensions of your universe - your life. Sit with your pain until you see it for what it really is and sit with your problems until you see them as information to absorb and understand, rather than something you need to control. Then step-by-step you learn how to embrace life by feeding wisdom, truth and light into your world, hence tearing down the prison of your mind.

Now your Problem-Solving Mind becomes a useful tool with flexible barriers, whereby knowledge serves only as a gauge that no longer creates unnecessary limitations. In fact it's quite the opposite when you learn how to let knowledge become part of the beautiful process of creating knowing.

Now you are on the journey of Truth and . . .

PHASE SIXTEEN

In the Truth nothing is a problem

In the Truth there are no limitations because the possibilities are infinite. This is the best way to describe it if you are still caught in the Construct. However, even this is not ideal because the Problem-Solving Mind struggles with the concept of infinity, as it sees everything as having a beginning and an end.

Interestingly neither are actually right in the Truth, because there is no such thing as time itself, everything just is. So, there are neither beginnings nor ends. A simple way to put it that may work for you, is to say that time becomes irrelevant as wanting becomes an unnecessary process and it is this mode of wanting that drives you to become addicted to the concept of time.

Just relax and try and embrace the notion that nothing is a problem; not even the events of life that you would have traditionally seen as disastrous. Then you can start to find the pathways that represent the truth of your journey, rather than the pathways that feed your obsessive and falsely placed desire to get what the mind wants.

Life tells us everything we need to know. This knowing is always there. We just have to learn to see it, trust it, and educate the mind with it.

Life's information is a light from the Universe that can illuminate the inside of your mind.

Knowledge, which is life's information not completely understood, will quickly turn into pain if it is not seen for what it is; so open up the parameters of your awareness and turn knowledge into knowing. Knowing is not a fixed intellectual notion, but rather a flexible place of sensory freedom.

Until you get on the awareness train, you will never truly understand whom you are. You will never be able to teach the Problem-Solving Mind to understand the nature of your existence and you will never go on the journey to the Unified Self.

The Problem-Solving Mind quite simply will never figure this out without the real you guiding it. For when it is left to its own devices, it becomes so obsessed with maintaining its beliefs for survival, all else becomes excluded from its functioning.

Hence, you will stay living in . . .

The Insanity of Humanity.

CONCLUSION

Utopia

CONCLUSION

I was born with compassion in my heart for all living beings and explored deeply the nature of life since a child. Always concerned for the suffering of others, I could see quite early on that many people were cruel and not behaving in a conscious manner. So my quest was to understand why, and on this journey it still took me many years to make the connections in my own behaviour that were indirectly linked to cruelty. This was mainly because society had disguised such conduct with images of happiness and good times. The fact that I 'missed' certain rather obvious links between behaviour and their outcomes seems almost ridiculous now, but conditioning since birth can be hard to see through and we are built not to change. Creating honest awareness requires a lot of conscious effort and exploration.

Unfortunately many of us have been lost in fear for so long that we are almost incapable of seeing beyond the beliefs that our current mode of existence creates. So whether we can 'wake' humanity up is questionable at best, but definitely possible. It will require the right information presented in such a manner that people's beliefs don't distort this information. Creating this scenario for people to 'have' to listen to such things is the real challenge, as we appear to still be resisting the entire truth of what our presence on this planet has created, hence we are not yet asking the right questions to handle this crisis. The movement of truth, compassion, honesty and intelligence lacks funds and strength within the individuals that are behind it, as they are all so emotionally depleted and few in number, and their personal lives are still reliant upon the systems that are creating the cruelty and madness that they wish to stop. So we all must do this together, as this time change will not happen via normal means that we have seen in the past – this time we must all change for real and soon.

I feel most people are fairly decent given the fear that they all live with, and they do not knowingly do great harm to other living beings. However, sadly, there are some people in this world that function with zero integrity and zero compassion for life, and they manipulate our repressed state of being. They are directly abusing life for personal gain and they can trust we will do little to stop them. In fact, because of our repressed state, they know they can profit from their cruel actions owing to the edited realities we live in. Meaning we are easy to manipulate because we have not been shown how to care beyond self and whatever is attached to that, hence feeling good becomes more important than truth. This is evidenced in the fact, and let me be clear that what I'm saying is fact not theory, that human beings contribute to the greatest tragedy of life on planet Earth. The greater part of the suffering is being worn by the many other species that we share this planet with - we murder unfathomable numbers of living beings every week for our pleasure, entertainment, convenience and profit. No, most of us are not doing the killing, but we appear happy to partake in the by-products without really even flinching. These animals are only being killed to satiate human wants, and all of this is completely unnecessary for our survival, and yet this we will defend and justify more than any other aspect of human behaviour once confronted. Thus the importance of NOT avoiding this topic, as it can, once understood, clear up all the confusion about everything to do with our destructive ways, including what we need to do to change.

So are we just a cruel species with little foresight, or are we trapped in a certain mode of thought that is destroying the planet and everything that inhabits it? As discussed in great length throughout the book, we certainly are trapped in a clearly identifiable system of functioning, created by the Problem Solving Mind, using fear as a guide. We are almost blind in the midst of this emotionally overwhelming experience, and this can only change by unleashing our compassion and expanding our realities by facing the truth of everything - not just what is convenient.

We have become so lost in our own pain that at times we cannot even recognize or feel the intense suffering of others. So we have a lot to look at and a lot to face, individually and collectively. I encourage you with all my heart to look deep into your own, and expand your love out beyond the things closest to you and afford the same love and compassion to every person/species that you encounter. For if we can learn to do this simple and obvious thing, we can learn to be the masters of our universe without needing to be the masters of domination and control, which would create societies with far less crime and violence.

I am sure I would be safe in saying that nearly every human being that has ever existed on planet Earth has dreamt of living in a state of Utopia and I am sure each of these individuals would be delighted to be in such a place of existence. However, we have not managed as a species to create Utopia. We end up getting lost in dreaming of such things, and at the same time never actually believing that this will happen, hence we make horrific allowances and justifications in our behaviour towards ourselves, other human beings and other species on this planet.

Aligned with the animal suffering, there are also large numbers of people living in horrendous conditions, struggling to meet the basic needs for the continuance of their lives. And in more 'civilized' societies people are suffering in very different ways – a huge portion of the human population have psychological conditions ranging from anxiety, to depression, to more advanced consequences of problem-solving. Because of this psychological suffering it is very difficult for any of us to truly feel for or care about anything other than ourselves, except perhaps, things very close to us, like family, friends or pets... and even this can be a struggle. It has gotten to the point where we can barely cope with our own survival; hence we do little towards creating the Utopia that we know must be built for our species to survive. In our existing way of being, we cannot connect our individual responsibility with the destruction of life that we are collectively creating. We share a distorted version of what is happening via our problem-solving pathways, so unfortunately the greater picture of life is never seen.

Somehow this situation we have found ourselves in has become acceptable and unfortunately this is destroying us from within. As

The Insanity of Humanity

we develop this illness in our mind, the illness we see in the outer world will increase; so one thing feeds the other and on goes the journey into the Insanity of Humanity and the psychological black hole of the human mind. So if we keep defending our outer actions connected to abuse, then of course we will never be able to see the corruption within our own self.

We must seriously stop and look at all of this as honestly as we can and start working towards creating a sustainable and compassionate world. Yes we adults have not had the pleasure, privilege and opportunity to grow up in such a way, and changing is hard, but that does not excuse us to inflict this on our children and to bring them up with the same insane behaviour that we are currently partaking in. It is almost too late for us to change and face the truth as adults, so can we really expect children to suddenly become compassionate, real, and honest, when we have not taught them to be this way? And the answer is obvious, no we can't. Do we need a generation of kind and wise people to lead us into the future? And the answer to that is an obvious yes!

If you're genuinely interested in life, your life, other people's lives, the lives of animals, and the sustainability of our environment, then we must all expand our realities to be able to connect on a far greater level with life then we currently do. If we were to do this, the love that we would, for example, afford our mother, would be the same love we would afford for all living beings. We would not justify abuse and our connection to it, allowing for a more compassionate expression of life. And even if we can't feel the pain and suffering of *everything*, we can at least logically know that it is offensive to our humanity to continue to do what we are doing. Our current pathways are destroying us at the very fabric of our existence. It is time for us to advance forward and to embrace the future with new eyes. Eyes of honesty and reason, and within that, compassion will come, because once we face the truth of what we are seeing, change will happen and we will create a sustainable world.

But we have to get out of our delusional state that continues to enforce a ridiculous notion that we can continue to be abusers of the planet and somehow expect Utopia to exist for us. To continue that way we will have to officially diagnose our entire species as completely insane and that this planet is nothing more than a holding ground for pure madness, as opposed to a birthplace for consciousness to come to life and to embrace this world with strength, intelligence, character, creativity and love.

Everything that I've written in this book is the starting point to ignite this journey. There is nothing that I have written that we do not have to face and understand, so my advice is that you read this book many times and maybe read a chapter and think about it while discussing it with a friend. Keep reading it and keep exploring it until you understand, at the very least, the logic behind what I have presented. If you decide to do nothing about changing your current destructive behaviours, you are effectively contributing to the demise of life on Earth, let alone your own life, your family's life, and generations into the future (if we make it that far). In the meantime, for those willing to look a little deeper, can you let the heinous reality that currently surrounds you continue? Because if we do collectively continue as we are, we must face at least one obvious truth, that this united journey is destroying our home and that it would be insane for us to not look deeper into the fabric of our behaviour, the very thing that is creating the destruction we are witnessing.

If this is sounding too depressing to face, relief is close at hand, because;

The truth can't hurt you, only your resistance to it.

For within this statement is the key to everything that could free humanity from its bondage and self-destructive ways. If we simply never defended anything, never problem-solved, and never tried to 'strategise' our lives; we would be able to absorb life in an un-edited state and we would now build the pathways of life through awareness rather than fear.

The power awareness has to heal the mind and release the true nature of *us* is simply amazing, as it affords humanity a peaceful exit from its pain, rather than everyone thinking that they must either run from it, or go deeper into it to find the clarity they seek. Pain, if explored, will expose the mechanisms of control, but it is a retractive energy, hence a destructive one, unlike awareness which is expansive.

Try this:

Next time you have a 'serious' discussion with your partner, friend or family member, try just listening to what they have to say about you, or any aspects of your life where strong beliefs are held. If you feel any 'heavy' emotions you know you are resisting. If this is the case just relax and listen again until you can stop fearing the truth – the truth that this person is saying what they feel, whatever that is, whether what they are saying is 'right' or 'wrong', it really makes no difference. If what they are sharing is important for you to hear, your non-defensive embracing of this information will trigger an internal healing process. There is nothing you actually have to 'do' to address the issue, as change will occur naturally and innately with little effort. And in doing this you have also expanded your reality which allows for more wisdom and vision to enter your life. With these come strength, confidence and an energy that attracts everything one needs to consciously evolve - rather than leading to a life of increased controls to attain what one wants.

Do you care to feel all of life, to see it for what it is, and then to discover the enormity of what we can become? If the answer is yes, then burst through your conditioning and allow yourself to see the truth of life, the most transformative journey you could ever take. It will free you from your psychological bondage ... what else could? Think about that ... a lot! Release every aspect of every moment, without defence or fear, whatever age you are, or wherever you're at in life. There is an expansive journey waiting for everyone but it must be ignited.

So if you 'want' to become addicted to something, become addicted to TRUTH, which of course once discovered as a way of being, is not an addiction at all, in fact the complete opposite. Truth allows for one's self to never be addicted to anything, as an addiction requires editing, and in the truth you are at one with life, you never resist life, as life is what it is, and this therefore leaves just you! So no more 'YOU' to figure out and hence the greatest stress of everyone's life is removed, which leaves energy for so much more in the expression of one's existence.

Uncover the truth, use the Internet, communicate honestly, explore and question the status quo, don't be a zombie and settle for nothing less than living in what is!

Never resist the truth no matter how offensive it is.

This will allow you to see the Insanity that has infected our Humanity!

To see truth as offensive is to be sitting in a defensive seat and that disallows the complete expansion of ones life. And always remember…

Nothing is a problem outside the limiting parameters of our life story.

See you in Utopia!

www.ingramcontent.com/pod-product-compliance
Lightning Source LLC
Chambersburg PA
CBHW032029290426
44110CB00012B/728